SPECIAL THANKS:

The authors wish to acknowledge the following individuals who contributed to the design and editing of **Die$mart** | diesmart.com.

Mike Barbarino, Robin Driscoll, Luther Knox, James Propp, Julie Propp
Minnie Scott, Dan Spector, Minna Vallentine, Tim Weir, Bill Lane & Mary Wright

Kathy Lane | Christine Hughes

Die$mart www.diesmart.com

Die$mart

Published by nFormed LLC
Half Moon Bay,CA
2011

ISBN 978-0-9821230-0-3

Design and Production By:
Knox Design and Propp+Guerin

Die$mart

Disclaimer:

The information provided in this book does not offer, and should not be construed as providing legal, accounting or tax advice or professional services to any individual or group of individuals. This is not a do-it-yourself book but rather a handbook providing useful information about matters related to death or incapacity. It may serve as a reference guide when you speak with attorneys or other professionals who can give personalized advice tailored to your particular situation or answer your specific questions.

While data contained in this material is gathered from sources believed to be reliable, accuracy and completeness cannot be guaranteed. Furthermore, the information contained in the book is current only up to the publication date and is likely to change. The authors, editor and the publisher shall have neither liability nor responsibility for any loss or damage caused, or alleged to have been caused, directly or indirectly, by the information contained in this book.

Die$mart www.diesmart.com

PROLOGUE

Here are the facts: You are going to die. You don't know when. You don't where. You don't know how. But it's going to happen.

Another fact: You may not die fast. 40% of us will die from Alzheimer's or other forms of dementia; 20% of us will die from cancer; and 20% of us will die from chronic cardiac or respiratory failure. That means 80% of us will die a lingering -- and probably expensive -- death.

Here's another fact -- and this one is really important. If you don't take charge and understand what can happen to you and your money, the state will take over and your loved ones will have to fight for your rights and intentions.

We are writing this book for you because we have lived the nightmare of "dying dumb." We faced losses, personal and financial, that should have never happened.

We took care of our parents and watched our friends take care of their spouses, partners or parents as caregivers and, finally, as executors of their estates.

When our parents died, we paid $9,000 in probate fees to get the right to sell a van worth $25,000. In our conversations with friends over dinner, we kept hearing "If only I had known." We found it hard to believe that educated people like ourselves did not understand the paperwork or the legal and financial aspects associated with dying.

We realized that nobody teaches someone how to die smart in school. Not only is the business side of death and dying a scary subject, it is shrouded in the mystery of complex laws and legal jargon, and we are told is something best left to "professionals". These laws cross multiple subjects and disciplines, including probate law, medical and retirement benefits laws, insurance, tax, and laws relating to the funeral industry.

Few of us understand the laws that manage our lives in case of disability or death, or really understand why the lack of planning means someone pays later. However, public cases like Terri Schiavo and Anna Nicole Smith demonstrate all too well the courts' willingness and obligation to make decisions for us when we can't.

Our personal experience taught us there are eleven common mistakes that cost us dearly. We don't want you to make those same mistakes. That's why we wrote this book.

Don't Just Die. Die Smart.
www.diesmart.com

CONTENTS

GETTING STARTED:

Let's face it. This could be complicated. There will be terms, documents and ideas that are new to you and that can be confusing.

To help you, we have organized the chapters as follows:

Each chapter begins with a list of terms discussed in that chapter, referred to as Words To Know. If some of the terms are unfamiliar to you, you can find an explanation of those words in the glossary.

Next comes an overview -- "What You Will Learn In This Chapter".

Each chapter contains at least one Family Story. Many are real life stories from our families and our friends to illustrate real life experiences. Family Stories are identified with the icon.

Facts provide interesting information particular to a specific topic and are identified by the fyi icon.

If you see an info **ibutton,** it identifies a subject where different states may have state or county specific rules, forms or fees. The state specific information can be found at **www.diesmart.com**/ibutton.

At the end of the chapter, we provide the Bottom Line, $ the consequences of making the mistakes. A checklist is also provided. By completing the action items listed in the checklist, you can truly die $mart.

Finally, since laws and legal processes change, we offer a companion web site, **www.diesmart.com**, to provide additional resources, sample forms and up to date information.

Mistake #1: You never even heard of Living Probate

Words to Know:

- Conservator
- Conservatorship
- DNR
- Durable Power of Attorney
- Funeral Agent
- Health Care Power of Attorney
- HIPPA
- In Case of Emergency ("ICE")
- Living Probate
- Living Will
- POLST
- Surety Bond
- Will

A Family Story: Living Probate.

Marsha waited in the intensive care unit where her husband was diagnosed with a life-threatening stroke. Roger, only 50 years old, no longer had the ability to speak, and will need physical therapy for the remaining years of his life.

Marsha decided to quit her job, sell the house she and Roger owned as joint tenants, and move to a smaller house with easier access for a wheelchair.

Marsha visited with the real estate agent. The real estate agent asked Marsha if Roger had completed a durable power of attorney form appointing Marsha as his financial agent.

Marsha said, "I don't understand. I don't know what a durable power of attorney is, and I am sure Roger has not completed one. I'm Roger's wife. Can't I just sign my name and Roger's name?"

Marsha discovered that in the eyes of the law, Roger was no longer authorized to make financial decisions for himself. Roger could not sell a house, sign a check, or even decide what type of health care he wanted. Marsha, his wife of 30 years, did not have the inherent right to make financial transactions on Roger's behalf.

The probate court is the "default person" with the right and obligation to oversee and appoint a conservator for someone like Roger, who could not make financial decisions on his own and who had not appointed someone to make financial decisions for him. Without such a conservator being appointed, no decisions could be made or contracts entered into regarding Roger.

The probate courts became involved in Marsha and Roger's lives while they were living, referred to by the legal profession as Living Probate.

Marsha had to first file documents with the probate court requesting a court hearing to determine Roger's ability to make decisions on his own. At this initial hearing, the probate judge considered declarations from physicians and other witnesses about Roger's physical and mental conditions.

Once the judge ruled that Roger was unable to make decisions on his own, Marsha was appointed as the conservator for Roger. The probate court issued documents known as Letters, empowering Marsha to act. Once Marsha obtained these Letters, Marsha had the legal authority to manage financial transactions on behalf of Roger and was able to put the house up for sale.

Before Marsha was appointed as the conservator, Marsha had to purchase a surety bond. The surety bond is a form of insurance guaranteeing the payment of money should Marsha wrongfully deprive Roger of his property.

As the court appointed conservator, Marsha had to file documents with the probate court listing all the assets owned by Roger. Marsha may need approval of the court before she can sell assets jointly owned with or owned by Roger.

Although the capacity declaration is confidential, all other documents filed with the probate court are public records. Anyone can see the documents describing Roger's and Marsha's financial assets.

Marsha spent almost $8,000 in legal fees to declare Roger incompetent and an additional $4,000 to be appointed the conservator for Roger. Marsha will have ongoing legal costs preparing and filing annual reports explaining how she managed Roger's financial assets. In addition, Marsha must pay a fee to renew the surety bond each year. This is living probate and it won't end until Roger dies.

WHAT YOU WILL LEARN IN THIS CHAPTER

As we age, we may need someone to help manage our money or make medical choices for us. The law gives each of us the right to document who we want to make these choices for us and what choices we want made. These documents are referred to as advance directives.

This chapter explains what types of advance directive forms are available and the consequences of not completing the forms.

WHY IS DYING DIFFERENT TODAY?

In 1900, the usual place of death was at home; in 2000, it was the hospital. In 1900, most people died in accidents or as a result of acute infections, and they rarely endured long periods of disability. In 2000, people spent, on average, two years severely disabled on the way to death. Acute causes of death (such as pneumonia and influenza) are in decline, whereas deaths from age-related, chronic, degenerative diseases (such as Alzheimer's, Parkinson's and emphysema) are on the rise.

A 2006 Rand study tried to envision the future needs of elderly people who are terminally ill, and classified the elderly into four groups:

- The first group will die after a short period of sharp decline. This is the typical course of death from cancer. Roughly 20 percent of all deaths are of this type.
- The second group will die following several years of increasing physical limitations, punctuated by intermittent acute life-threatening episodes. This is the typical course of death from chronic cardiac or respiratory failure. Roughly 20 percent of all deaths are of this type.
- The third—and the largest—group will only die after prolonged dwindling, usually lasting many years. This is the typical course of death from dementia (including Alzheimer's disease) and disabling stroke. The trajectory towards death is gradual but unrelenting, with steady decline, enfeeblement and growing dependency, often lasting a decade or longer. Roughly 40 percent of all deaths are projected to be of this type.
- The other 20 percent will die as a result of some sudden and acute event, like an accident.

Source: Federal Government Study: "The Dilemma of an Aging Society"

These facts are astonishing. Eighty percent of us need to make planning for incapacity just as important as planning for death.

WHAT ARE ADVANCE DIRECTIVES?

If your mental capacity becomes compromised as you age, or if you suffer an unexpected accident or illness, your spouse or your children may need to help manage your finances or your health care. Sounds simple? It's not. The fact is incapacity, like dying, is an event in your life where laws decide who has the authority to manage your affairs for you when you can't. These are the laws your family and friends will be required to follow if you become unable to make decisions on your own behalf.

As an example, when your children talk with your doctor, they will find the doctor requires a health care power of attorney signed by you giving one of your children the legal authority to make health care choices for you. Your spouse will discover he or she does not have the authority to sell a house you jointly own unless you have completed a durable power of attorney form appointing him or her as your attorney-in-fact.

The law recognizes the legal rights of a competent adult to leave instructions on what choices you want made regarding your health care and your finances and to appoint someone you trust to carry out those wishes.

- You can complete a health care power of attorney form appointing someone you trust to make health care choices for you.
- You can complete a living will form documenting your end of life wishes.
- You can complete a durable power of attorney form appointing someone you trust with the power to act as your financial agent.

If you become physically incapacitated or are considered mentally incompetent, the law considers you unable to make decisions for yourself.

- If you have not completed forms appointing someone to make choices for you when you can't, your family may need to involve the probate court to request and get authority to act on your behalf. For a fee.

- If you have failed to make appropriate advance instructions or your instructions are incomplete, the court appointed agent will follow whatever instructions are provided for in your state laws.

Your family will find they need multiple documents to act on your behalf, each one serving a different purpose. The following group of questions and answers can help you understand what documents are needed and what purpose they serve.

Fact: Incapacity can happen to anyone.

Although planning for death is important, planning for mental or physical incapacity is just as important. A recent government study stated "eighty percent of people over the age of 65 will spend one to ten years under the care of a caregiver". In less than two decades it is expected that some 30 million people will suffer from some form of dementia. If this happens to you, someone must manage your health care and your money.

Source: Federal government report: "The Dilemma of an Aging Society"

Planning is not just for the elderly. Terri Schiavo was 26 years old when she had a heart attack and slipped into a "permanent vegetative" condition. She then lived for fourteen years until she was allowed to die following enormous expenses to her family while incapacitated.

WHO WILL MAKE HEALTH CARE CHOICES FOR YOU IF YOU CANNOT?

Health Care Power of Attorney (HCPOA) or Health Care Directive

You can complete a health care power of attorney form and name a health care agent to make health care choices for you if and when you can't. This person will make sure your previously written wishes relating to your health care are carried out. This agent may also request other treatments for you consistent with your broad directives regarding your health care.

Some states call this document a health care proxy. Some states call your health care agent a health care surrogate. Some states combine the health care power of attorney form with the living will form in a single document referred to as an advanced health care directive.

Fact: Advanced Health Care Directive.

These states have adopted the use of an advanced health care directive, a single form documenting your end of life choices and your designation of a health care agent: Alabama, Arizona, California, Connecticut, Delaware, District of Columbia, Hawaii, Kentucky, Minnesota, Mississippi, Nevada, New Jersey, New Mexico, Oklahoma, Oregon, Pennsylvania and Virginia.

The person you identify as your agent when you complete your health care power of attorney will be empowered to give informed consent on your behalf, and may make decisions about whether you should undergo medical procedures or elect hospice care.

The more specific you make your instructions regarding your health care choices, the better. These instructions should address whether your agent has the authority to withhold artificial resuscitation, hydration and nutrition, depending on your circumstance. In many states, the Health Care Power of Attorney is a "statutory form," meaning the authority granted to your health care agent and the signature requirements are specifically described in state law. **ibutton:** Health Care Power of Attorney diesmart.com/ibutton

info

Q. *Who should you appoint as your health care agent?*

A. There is no limitation on who you may name as your health care agent. It could be your spouse, an adult child, another relative or a friend. We have found that your agent should, ideally, be a fighter: a person willing to make sure your wishes are carried out.

While you can only have one health care agent at a time, you may name a contingent agent in the event that the first person is unable or unwilling to serve.

Don't appoint someone without first asking if they are willing to serve as your health care agent and unless you trust them to carry out your health care wishes.

Q. *How long is a health care power of attorney effective?*

A. With one exception, the authority of the health care agent ends at your death when a personal representative, executor or a trustee takes over. The exception is that a person acting under a Health Care Power of Attorney could have been given authority to handle the final arrangements regarding your remains and funeral.

You can create a revocation form terminating the appointment of your health care agent at any time while you are living. **ibutton:** Health Care Power of Attorney Revocation Form www.diesmart.com/ibutton

info

Q. *What if you have not completed a health care power of attorney?*

A. If you are married or have a registered domestic partner, generally your spouse or registered domestic partner has the inherent legal right to make health care choices for you if you are unable to do so, even if you have not completed a health care power of attorney form.

If you have no spouse or registered domestic partner and become unable to manage your own personal health care decisions, someone will request the probate court to appoint a conservator who will be in charge of making health care decisions for you.

Your medical choices can be delayed unless you have legally identified a health care agent to make choices for you.

Fact: A single adult child also needs a health care power of attorney.

Parents of injured Virginia Tech students rushed to be at the side of their children. If their child was over 18 and had not signed a health care power of attorney, they found they did not have the legal authority to make health care choices for their child.

If your adult child is attending college, or is not married, your adult child should complete a health care power of attorney designating a parent or another adult as their health care agent.

WHAT ARE YOUR END OF LIFE WISHES?

Living Will

A living will is a document that sets out, in writing, your wishes in the event that you become terminally ill and there is no reasonable expectation of recovery. Some people ask to be kept alive as long as it is possible. Other people prefer that if there is no reasonable expectation of recovery, they no longer want to live. You can even elect not to make a choice regarding whether or not you want to receive life-sustaining medical treatment, and delegate this decision to your appointed health care agent.

If you are well enough, you can tell your doctors what types of medical treatment you want or don't want. If you can't speak, a living will describes what you want done or not done if you are terminally ill with no likelihood of recovery.

Almost all states have specific living will statutes. Most states without living will statutes recognize living wills, but may rely on the court decisions on the intent of the instructions contained in your living will.

Fact: States without living will statutes.

Currently, these states do not have living will statutes: Massachusetts, Missouri and New York. This does not mean if you live in one of these states that you should not have a living will. Your living will continues to provide evidence of your intentions.

Q. *Why do you need to complete both a durable health care power of attorney and a living will?*

A. A living will answers the question: What do you want done if you are being kept alive through an artificial life support system? Do you want to be kept alive at all costs or would you prefer to be allowed to die if there is no reasonable likelihood that you will ever get better? No matter which choice you make, state laws assure that you will continue to receive medical or other treatment available to alleviate pain.

A durable health care power of attorney (DHCPOA) answers the question: Who do you want to make decisions about your health care if you can't? If you have chosen to be allowed to die, a DHCPA empowers your health care agent to decide to withhold treatment.

Both documents are important parts of pre-death planning. A living will is a document relatively narrow in scope—it only applies to those circumstances described in the document. In contrast, a durable health care power of attorney vests a person with types of authority to make various decisions, and thus applies to a wider range of potential health care circumstances and decisions.

Q. *What if you have not completed a living will and you are facing a lingering death attached to machinery that is only keeping your vital organs alive?*

A. In the absence of a health care power of attorney or a living will, sometimes a physician will work with the spouse or family to carry out your wishes if the spouse and/or all members of the family agree on what to do.

Often, legal problems occur when family members do not agree on what was your intent and what should be done to carry out that intent.

Some state statutes specify who has the right to make health care choices for you if you have not identified a health care agent, usually a spouse, adult children or parents. Some states only require the consent of one person; some states require unanimous consent from adult children or parents. Without consensus, doctors have no choice but to provide life sustaining treatment.

A Family Story: Terri Schiavo.

Terri Schiavo suffered severe brain damage in 1990 after her heart stopped because of a chemical imbalance that was believed to have been brought on by an eating disorder. Terri was 26 years old. Court-appointed doctors ruled she was in a persistent vegetative state, with no real consciousness or chance of recovery.

The case focused national attention on living wills, since Terri Schiavo left no written instructions in case she became disabled. Michael, Terri's husband, wanted to remove her feeding tube and let Terri die. Michael argued that his wife would not have wanted to live in her condition. Terri's parents wanted to keep Terry alive and argued she would want to be kept alive.

The courts became involved. The case spiraled through the court system for seven years, eventually being heard by the Supreme Court. The Supreme Court ruled that the husband had the right to decide and he subsequently had his wife taken off life support.

Do Not Resuscitate (DNR)

A Do Not Resuscitate (DNR) order is another kind of advance directive. A DNR is a request not to have cardiopulmonary resuscitation (CPR) if your heart stops or if you stop breathing. Unless paramedics or other emergency staff are given other instructions, paramedics and hospital staff will try to resuscitate any patient whose heart has stopped or who has stopped breathing.

The exact rules for obtaining a DNR and for proving its validity vary widely from state to state. **ibutton:** State DNR Rules www.diesmart.com/ibutton

Once you complete a DNR, make sure your physician and others are aware of your wishes. Give a copy of your DNR to your primary physician and request this information be added as part of your medial records. If you are in a hospital, make sure a copy of your DNR is included with your medical chart. Keep a copy of the original in your estate planning files.

Generally, doctors and hospitals in all states respect DNR orders.

Q. *If you have a heart attack or other medical condition that would appear to compromise your mental abilities, how do you tell someone you don't want to be resuscitated?*

A. Once your mental capacity has been substantially compromised, it is possible for a physician to determine that you lack sufficient mental capacity to provide informed medical consent.

If the physician considers that your mental capacity is diminished, it will be too late for you to instruct the medical staff not to resuscitate you. These orders must be made when you are healthy.

Q. *Why do you need to complete a living will and a DNR?*

A. The directions in your living will are only followed when your doctor believes you are in a terminal state and will not recover from your illness or injury. The directions in your DNR are effective the moment you sign them and do not require any type of medical condition to be present for the DNR to be effective.

Elderly people sometimes want a DNR if they suffer from chronic illnesses and are concerned that their quality of life will suffer if they require resuscitation.

Q. *What happens if the paramedics do not know y you have completed a DNR?*

A. If the paramedics or other medical personnel cannot locate your DNR, they will make an effort to save your life.

You can help the paramedics make the right treatment choices in several ways:

- Participate in the Vial of Life program. The Vial of Life program is a nationwide effort to assist emergency personnel to administer proper medical treatment for you when you can't speak for yourself.

  A Vial of Life sticker is placed on your door. This sticker tells the paramedic to look for your DNR and other medical information in a vial placed in your refrigerator. **ibutton:** Vial of Life www.diesmart.com/ibutton

- Some people recommend storing the DNR in the freezer in a blue freezer bag, as paramedics are trained to look in the freezer for DNR documents stored in a blue bag.

- Some states authorize the use of identification bracelets or tags as a way for you to notify medical personnel that you have signed a DNR. Although all states authorize the use of a DNR, some states require special paper to be used when printing as a means of authentication.

The exact rules for obtaining a DNR and for proving its validity vary widely from state to state. **ibutton:** Do Not Resuscitate www.diesmart.com/ibutton.

info

info

A Family Story: No DNR present.

Kathy's 92-year old mother was at her house watching TV when her mother suddenly said she could not breathe. Kathy called an ambulance.

As the paramedic prepared to take her mother to the hospital, Kathy explained to the paramedic that she and her mother had decided not to resuscitate if the situation was such that her mother's quality of life could be impaired.

The paramedic asked to see the DNR form. Kathy replied the form was at her mother's house in another state and was not able to provide a copy to the paramedic. The paramedic said they were allowed to wait sixty seconds for someone to provide the DNR. After that, they are required by law to administer all available life saving techniques.

Kathy now keeps a copy of the DNR in her freezer and in her purse. Her mother wears a DNR bracelet.

Physician Order for Life Sustaining Treatment (POLST)

Q. *What is POLST?*

A. POLST is a new program designed to improve the quality of care people receive at the end of their life and ensure a patient's wishes are fulfilled.. In some states it is called a Medical Orders for Life Sustaining treatment (MOLST).

The physician, after talking with the patient and the family, documents what type of end of life care is desired. It includes the patient's desire to have or refuse CPR, comfort measures, and whether to receive artificial nutrition. The document is valid in a nursing home, at home, in a long-term care facility, and in the hospital.

Currently, California, Hawaii, New York, Oregon, North Carolina, Tennessee, Washington and West Virginia have adopted state wide forms and procedures. Numerous other states are developing similar programs.

Q. *How does POLST different from other advance directives?*

A. A living will covers your wishes regarding all future medical situations. A POLST is specific to a certain time and specific medical situation.

The POLST form is a medical order and is completed and signed by a health care professional, usually a doctor or a nurse

An advance health care directive is not a medical order and is completed and signed by an individual.

WHO DO YOU WANT TO ACCESS YOUR MEDICAL RECORDS?

Health Information Privacy and Portability Act (HIPPA)

Q. *What is HIPPA?*

A. HIPPA is the acronym for the Health Insurance Portability and Accountability Act passed in 2003. In an effort to protect your privacy, HIPPA restricts the freedom of medical care providers to share medical information about you with anyone, even family members, without your consent.

The provisions of HIPPA give you the right to view information contained in your medical records and to designate other persons with whom your medical information may be shared.

Q. *Do you need to complete a HIPPA form in order for your spouse or family to see copies of your medical records?*

A. If you want your medical information shared with someone, you must complete a HIPPA Authorization to Release Information form naming and authorizing the people you wish to see the records maintained by your physician or hospital. Access to these records will be important for whoever is in charge of making medical decisions for you.

The list should certainly include your health care agent. Whether you want your medical information shared with your family is up to you. If you have old and trusted friends to whom you frequently turn for advice, you may want to name them as well.

Once you sign a HIPPA Authorization to Release Information form, you should give a copy to your family physician.

Although you can add a clause to your health care power of attorney form giving your health care agent and family access to your personal medical records, it is also wise to sign a separate HIPPA form identifying the people whom you want to have access to your records.

Q. *What if you have not completed a HIPPA form giving someone the legal right to view your medical records?*

A. Without a written authorization from you to share your medical records, medical professionals and medical facilities face stiff penalties for violating HIPPA.

Without advanced authorization by you, your health care agent, spouse, family and others will not be able to access the information about you to make an informed decision about the best plan of care for you.

Fact: HIPPA and adult children.

If an adult has a child attending college, they should consider having the child sign a HIPPA form giving their parent the right to access their medical records. Otherwise, if the student is in an accident, the parent may not have the right to view the child's medical records to make decisions about their care.

WHO WOULD YOU WANT CALLED IN CASE OF EMERGENCY (ICE)?

Q. *What is ICE?*

A. If you are in a car accident or some other event requiring unexpected medical care, the physicians and emergency personnel must find a way to contact someone regarding your medical emergency. Time is important. Some medical procedures require authorization from a spouse or a health care agent before treatment can begin. A shorthand process has been developed to facilitate this communication process, referred to as ICE. ICE stands for In Case of Emergency.

Q. *How Does ICE Work?*

A. ICE reflects the list of persons who you want contacted in case of an emergency. This list of persons and their telephone numbers (and other information) is stored on your cell phone. The steps are as follows:

- Decide whom you want contacted in case of emergency.

- Enter ICE as the contact name in your cell phone contact list.
- Add the phone number of the person you want called in case of emergency.
- If you want to name more than one person, make an ICE1 and ICE2 entry in your contact list.

Paramedics and other emergency responders are trained to examine your cell phone and look under "ICE" to see who ought to be contacted to give your location and condition.

WHO WILL MANAGE YOUR MONEY AND PROPERTY IF YOU CANNOT?

Durable power of Attorney

A durable power of attorney is a legal document you complete in which you appoint and delegate to an agent the power to make financial decisions and transactions on your behalf if you are unable to do so yourself.

The person you appoint in this document to act on your behalf is referred to as your attorney-in-fact.

A durable power of attorney gives the attorney-in-fact you name the power to make decisions other than health care choices for you if you can't. The term "durable" means the power of attorney form remains effective if you become incapacitated.

Some states call this document a "financial power of attorney" or "financial proxy." Some states call the attorney-in-fact an agent.

Just as important as naming someone to act as your agent is defining what powers you want to give to your agent.

Like your health care power of attorney, the more specific you are regarding the duties you want your agent to perform for you, the better. For example, your durable power of attorney should address whether your agent has the authority to write and deposit checks, buy or sell real estate, invest your money, manage your taxes and retirement accounts, borrow money, make gifts on your behalf, sign contracts that buy or sell things for you, change beneficiaries, hire counsel and engage in litigation on your behalf.

In many states, the durable power of attorney is a "statutory form," meaning the authority granted to your attorney-in-fact and the signature requirements are specifically described in state laws. When completing your power of attorney, understand what authority your state automatically grants your attorney-in-fact. It may be necessary for you to add language giving your agent certain powers or your agent will not have them.

- In New York, Florida and North Carolina, you must file a copy of your signed durable power of attorney with the county recorder where you own real estate if the power of attorney authorizes the attorney-in-fact to conduct real estate transactions. The document becomes a public record.

- Many states require that for an agent acting under a durable power of attorney to amend, modify or terminate a trust, both the durable power of attorney and the trust agreement must specifically provide this authority to the agent.

Q. *Who should you appoint as your attorney-in-fact?*

A. You can appoint an adult person or a financial institution to act as your attorney-in-fact.

You may name back-up agents in the event that the first person is unable or unwilling to serve. This is highly advisable. If you only name one agent and for some reason they can't act as your financial agent, your family will need to request the probate courts to appoint a financial agent to act on your behalf.

Q. *How long is a durable power of attorney effective?*

A. The authority of the attorney-in-fact generally ends at your death at which point a personal representative, executor or a trustee takes over.

You can create a revocation form terminating the appointment of your financial agent at any time while you are living. **ibutton:** Durable Power of Attorney Revocation Form www.diesmart.com/ibutton

Q. *Must your attorney-in-fact be an attorney?*

A. No. Your attorney-in-fact can be any adult person or financial institution, including your attorney. Financial institutions and attorneys-at-law usually charge a fee for serving as your attorney-in-fact. Some states require the person you appoint as your agent to also sign the durable power of attorney form, acknowledging their appointment.

Your attorney-in-fact should be someone you trust to manage your money when no one is watching them.

Fact: Your wife now is your ex-wife.

Some states provide that, upon divorce, the ex-spouse identified in a durable power of attorney as your attorney-in-fact is presumed to no longer be a valid selection as an attorney-in-fact. If you re-marry, be sure to amend your power of attorney form to identify your new spouse as your agent, assuming you believe the new spouse is the correct attorney-in-fact for you.

Q. *Can you appoint more than one attorney-in-fact?*

A. Generally, you may appoint more than one agent under a durable power of attorney. However, if you appoint two or more persons to simultaneously serve as your attorneys-in-fact, you should specify whether they must act jointly or whether each can act separately.

You may specify that for some types of decisions they must act together, and that for other types of decisions they may act separately. You might, for example, want both attorneys-in-fact to make the decision to sell your house, but allow either to manage your living expenses. If you own a business, you may consider creating a separate power of attorney to designate someone to make financial decisions about your business.

Q. *What is a "springing" power of attorney?*

A. A signed durable power of attorney is effective immediately, and stays effective until you revoke it or you die. You may add language to a durable power of attorney turning it into a "springing" power of attorney.

A "springing" power of attorney is not immediately effective. It "springs" into effect upon the happening of a specific event, such as illness or injury.

You can include language requiring your physician or a third party to confirm your mental incompetence to activate the power. This will give you some protection against a greedy or impatient attorney-in-fact. It will, unfortunately, delay the moment when somebody will be authorized to manage your affairs. You may add language to a durable power of attorney turning it into a "springing" power of attorney.

Not all states permit a springing power of attorney.
ibutton: Springing Power of Attorney www.diesmart.com/ibutton

info

Q. *If you have a living trust, do you need to complete a durable power of attorney form?*

A. Yes, you probably do. Your trust should include language granting the successor trustee or the co-trustee the right to make financial decisions regarding trust assets if you become legally incapacitated. When this language is part of the trust, the trustee has the right to manage trust property without any other legal procedures.

Even if you have a living trust where the language gives the trustee the right to manage trust assets on your behalf if you become incapacitated, it is almost certain that you will have some assets that are not owned by the trust, such as Individual Retirement Accounts (IRAs) or Roth retirement accounts.

Or you may own property whose title has not yet been transferred into the trust. Since these assets are not owned by the trust, the trustee of your trust and any instructions regarding incapacity in your living trust do not govern them.

Your durable power of attorney will give the attorney-in-fact the authority to manage property not owned by your trust. Your attorney-in-fact can be given authority, or instructed, to transfer all of your property to your living trust.

Q. *What is the difference between a durable power of attorney and a power of attorney?*

A. There is one key difference between the two. A power of attorney is effective if, at the time it is used, you are living and of sound mind. It ceases to be effective if you are dead or not of sound mind.

A durable power of attorney continues to be effective whatever your legal capacity, or incapacity, may be.
A durable power of attorney includes words such as

"This power of attorney shall not be impacted by any subsequent incapacity or disability".

Q. *How does your attorney-in-fact perform business on your behalf?*

A. Your agent would provide a copy of your signed, witnessed, and in some instances, notarized power of attorney form to your bank or brokerage firm. He or she would then sign documents on your behalf as "John Doe, attorney-in-fact for John Smith."

Some banks or financial institutions are reluctant to accept a power of attorney form. Ask your bank or financial institution the method in which someone can perform business on your behalf. If they ask you to complete a power of attorney form supplied by the bank, make sure the word "durable" is on the form.

A Family Story: Durable Power of Attorney.

Tom executed a durable power of attorney document, designating Katie, his wife, as his attorney-in-fact. As the named attorney-in-fact, Katie had the legal authority to make decisions for and on behalf of Tom.

Tom had a stroke six months later and was unable to communicate.

Katie decided to sell the house she and Tom owned as joint tenants. The Contract of Sale listed Katie and Tom as owners of the property. Signature lines were provided for both Katie and Tom to sign.

Katie signed as Katie. She then provided a copy of the power of attorney appointing Katie as the attorney-in-fact for Tom. Katie then signed on the line requiring Tom's signature as "Katie Smith, attorney-in-fact for Tom."

Q. *Does the agent you named in a durable power of attorney have the right to manage your health care decisions?*

A. In most states, the answer is no. State statutes governing financial power of attorneys do not permit the inclusion of language giving your agent the right to also manage your health care. You must create a separate health care power of attorney form identifying the person you want to make health care choices for you when you can't.

Fact: Power of attorney statutes.

If you live in Alaska or Pennsylvania, statutes allow you to add instructions to your financial power of attorney covering your health care decisions.

Q. *What happens if you have not completed a durable power of attorney?*

A. If you become incapacitated and have not properly created a durable power of attorney, it is likely that no one has the legal authority to make financial transactions on your behalf without court intervention.

- It surprises many married couples to learn that a spouse does not have the legal authority to buy or sell property without their spouse appointing them as their financial agent.
- If your children need to act as caregivers, your children may not be able to manage your money without you designating them as your attorney-in-fact.

- If you are not married, your partner will generally not have the legal right to manage your financial affairs unless you have completed a power of attorney naming your partner as your attorney-in-fact.

In the absence of any such advance directive from you giving someone the power to manage your money and property for you, a spouse, child, attorney, or other relative or must begin a legal process known as a Conservatorship with the probate court.

Q. *What happens when a conservatorship case is filed?*

A. Conservatorship is a judicial process whereby the probate court appoints a person, referred to as a conservator, to hold and protect your personal and financial rights.

The purpose of the conservatorship process is to have the probate court appoint someone and give them legal authority to make financial decisions and/or personal care decisions on your behalf. Some states call this process a Guardianship, as the person appointed to take care of a mentally incompetent adult has duties similar to those of a guardian for a minor or disabled child.

Attorneys often refer to the conservatorship process as living probate, because the probate courts become involved in managing your affairs while you are living.

The conservatorship process is a two-part procedure.

Step 1: Someone, usually a spouse or an adult child, must file documents with the courts requesting you be declared incapable of managing your personal or business affairs.

When a conservatorship action is filed, it must be served on all interested parties. The court will set a time for an evidentiary hearing. At the hearing, testimony will be given by friends and medical professionals regarding your physical and mental health. You may be present at the hearing and the judge may ask you questions to establish your incompetence.

After hearing the evidence, the court may deem you mentally incompetent and/or unable to care for your own basic personal and financial protection.

Step 2: After the court agrees you are incapable of managing your own affairs, your spouse or some other third party will request they be appointed as conservator.

More than one party may apply to serve as your conservator. If there is more than one person who seeks to be appointed conservator, state preference laws give higher priority to the appointment based on their relation to you. For example, if you are married, the preference is for your spouse. If you are not married, the next priority is usually your parents. Other interested parties, including members of your family, have the right to contest a request to act as your conservator.

The person appointed to act on your behalf, referred to as the conservator, is required by law to provide to the court an accounting of how they manage and spend your money. The conservator can charge a fee for performing these duties. All legal, accounting and court fees are paid for from assets owned by you, the conservatee.

A Family Story: Living Probate: Contested Conservatorship.

Matt and Emma, a married couple, owned a restaurant together. Matt had been married before; he had one daughter from that marriage, Jessica, age 28.

Matt, at the age of 57, suffered a stroke, from which he suffered major brain damage rendering him incapable to walk, talk or think rationally. Matt's doctors concluded his condition was permanent. Emma decided to sell the business and take care of Matt.

Matt had not prepared a durable power of attorney. No one had the legal authority to sign any documents authorizing the sale of the business.

Emma met with her lawyer. The lawyer explained the need to file for a conservatorship over Matt.

Emma filed documents requesting the court declare Matt incompetent and for her to be appointed as the conservator. The court scheduled a time to hear testimony from Matt's doctors. Emma and Jessica attended the hearings. The judge agreed Matt was incompetent and needed someone to make decisions on his behalf.

Jessica contested the appointment of Emma as the conservator and filed documents alleging such a choice would put Jessica's inheritance at risk.

After a lengthy, expensive, public legal procedure, the court appointed a financial institution as the "conservator of the estate" for Matt. This financial institution will receive a fee for managing Matt's affairs, money which will come from Matt's income. The court appointed Emma the "conservator of the person" for Matt.

All of the documents filed with the courts regarding Matt's physical condition and his finances are public information.

Just when Matt needs the support of both Emma and Jessica, they are not talking to each other.

Matt could have executed a power of attorney naming Jessica and Emma as co-attorneys-in-fact, requiring both signatures on financial decisions. This simple document would have likely eliminated costly legal proceedings and the management of Matt's financial affairs by someone Jessica and Emma have never met.

Q. *Can you prevent your financial or health care information filed with the courts from being public?*

A. Documents filed with the courts as part of a Conservatorship procedure are generally public records. Anyone can visit a probate court or go on line and review most of these documents.

WHO WOULD YOU LIKE TO NAME AS YOUR CONSERVATOR?

Pre-Need Guardian

Sometimes, whether you like it or not, someone may file documents with the probate court requesting the courts appoint a conservator to act on your behalf. Anyone is entitled to seek to have you conserved or to have a guardian appointed for you.

In such a case, if you have previously completed a pre-need guardian form and designated a person who you trust to serve as your conservator or guardian, the court will give first priority to that person in its appointment. If you have not prepared a pre-need guardian form, the court may appoint someone you would not want making financial and health care choices for you.

Some states allow you to file this form with the Clerk of the Court. **ibutton:** Pre-Need Guardian Forms by State www.diesmart.com/ibutton.

Fact: Pre-Need Guardian for minor children.

If you have minor children, you should also complete a Pre-Need Guardian form designating someone you want to become your children's guardian, in case you ever become incapacitated. This document may not deny a natural parent their right to be a custodian, but single parents should complete this form. See Mistake #10 for more information regarding minor children and guardians.

WHAT OTHER SIGNATURE FORMS ARE NEEDED TO MANAGE YOUR FINANCIAL AFFAIRS?

Certain assets have special rules regarding the appointment of a financial agent to manage your money and property.

Social Security

Q. *How would you give someone the right to manage your social security payments?*

A. Treasury department regulations do not permit a power of attorney or a durable power of attorney to be used to manage your social security benefits. A family member or other person must complete a Social Security Representative Payee form designating a "representative payee" to act on your behalf regarding social security benefits.

Social Security will then send your social security benefits to the representative payee. The representative payee is required to prepare and file an annual report describing how they spent the money on your behalf.

The representative payee is also obligated to report any change in circumstances impacting your eligibility to receive social security benefits. **ibutton:** Representative Payee reporting form www.diesmart.com/ibutton

Brokerage Accounts

Q. *How will your attorney-in-fact be able to manage your brokerage accounts?*

A. Brokerage accounts have special rules for your attorney-in-fact.

If your attorney-in-fact needs to buy or sell stocks held in physical form or held in a brokerage account, your attorney-in-fact will need to add a medallion signature "guarantee" to their power of attorney form.

The medallion signature is a stamp provided by a

financial institution guaranteeing to a transfer agent that the signature of your attorney-in-fact is actually their signature.

Requests to buy or sell stocks are reviewed by someone referred to as a Transfer Agent. The Transfer Agent cannot authorize transactions requested by your attorney-in-fact without the medallion signature guarantee evident on the power of attorney form.

Your attorney-in-fact may need to locate a bank participating in the medallion signature program. The bank should be one the attorney-in-fact does business with that is willing to guarantee its signature. The bank puts the medallion stamp on the power of attorney form.

Safe Deposit Box

Q. *How will your attorney-in-fact get access to your safe deposit box?*

A. If you open a safe deposit box in the name of your trust, the trustee or successor trustee has the legal right to access the safe deposit box.

When you open a safe deposit box in your name, or as a joint tenant, ask whether your bank will accept your power of attorney as authorization for your attorney-in-fact to access your safe deposit box.

Some banks will not. These banks may require you to complete a separate form they provide designating a safe deposit box agent. The box renters will complete the form naming a safe deposit box agent in the presence of a bank employee, which gives the bank greater assurance about the validity of the authorization.

Banks and other financial institutions struggle with accepting your power of attorney. Currently, there is no way for banks to know if you have revoked your power of attorney or changed the name of your attorney-in-fact.

WHO DO YOU WANT TO MANAGE YOUR FUNERAL ARRANGEMENTS?

Nominating A Funeral Agent

Before you die, you have the legal right to appoint a funeral agent who will become responsible for carrying out and/or planning your funeral wishes.

This person has the right to decide: (a) whether you will be cremated or buried with your body intact and (b) where to bury your body or your ashes.

Q. *How do you appoint a funeral agent?*

A. The document you use to appoint a funeral agent is dependent upon the state you live in.

- Some states require that you appoint a funeral agent in your will.
- Some states provide that the attorney-in-fact named on your power of attorney may act as your funeral agent.
- Some states have created a new form entitled, "Disposition of Remains" giving you the right to name a funeral agent and specify whether you want your body cremated, buried intact, or donated to medical research. **ibutton:** Funeral Agent Rules By State www.diesmart.com/ibutton

info

Q. *What happens if you don't appoint a funeral agent?*

A. State preference laws entitle a surviving family member to act as your funeral agent and give that family member the right to make choices regarding the disposition of your body.

A Family Story: Domestic partners.

Susan and Linda had lived together as partners for many years in the state of Kansas. Linda named Susan as the executor in her will, but did not include instructions giving Susan the right to make funeral arrangements.

When Linda was diagnosed with cancer, Susan assumed the caregiver role. In talking with Susan, Linda expressed her desire to be cremated and have her ashes buried at sea.

Linda died. Linda's mother wanted Linda to be buried with her body intact and next to her father. State preference laws in Kansas gave Linda's mother the right to make choices regarding the disposition of Linda's body.

Susan expressed Linda's desires to Linda's mother, to no avail. Linda was buried in Kansas.

Q. *What information should you provide your agent regarding your funeral wishes?*

A. At a minimum, you should leave instructions specifying:

- Whether you want to be buried with your body intact, cremated, or have your body donated for medical research. If you want your body donated for medical research, you should sign an agreement with a medical research institution before you die. Your family or funeral agent may not have the legal authority to donate your body for medical research after you die.
- Where you want your body to be buried, or have your ashes scattered.

- How you would like your life celebrated, if at all.
- Whether or not you have prepaid for your funeral or a cemetery plot.
- Whether or not you want to participate in the organ and tissue donation program. If you don't document your wishes, your family has the right to make this choice for you.
- Whether you have already taken and stored a sample of your DNA, or want a DNA sample taken before disposing of your body.

You can find more information and resources for planning your funeral at **ibutton:** Funerals diesmart.com/ibutton

info

Bottom Line:

Planning for incapacity is as important as planning for death.

It's Your Choice.

- You can either document your wishes or your health care agent must follow the instructions of the state where you live regarding life support.
- You can name someone you trust to manage your finances and make health care choices for you, or the state can appoint someone you don't even know to make choices for you. For a fee.

Action Checklist: Avoid Living Probate.

- ❑ Complete a durable power of attorney or living trust. Avoid the costs and emotional trauma involved with Living Probate.
- ❑ Complete a living will and a durable health care power of attorney.
- ❑ Designate a funeral agent to carry out your funeral wishes.
- ❑ Complete and carry a DNR with you.
- ❑ Store your emergency contact information on your cell phone under ICE.
- ❑ Place the Vial of Life sticker on your door. Place your medical information in a vial in your refrigerator.
- ❑ Prepare a Pre-Need Guardian Form or otherwise name and identify a person who you wish to serve as your guardian or conservator and/or your minor child's guardian in case of incapacity.
- ❑ Document whether or not you want to participate in the organ or tissue donation program.

Mistake #2: You trusted Medicare to pay for long term care

Words to Know:

- CLASS
- Long Term Care
- Long Term Care Insurance
- Medicaid
- Medicaid Estate Recovery
- Medicaid Look Back
- Medicaid Penalty Period
- Medicare

A Family Story: Medicare does not pay for long term care.

Esther was one of eleven children raised on a farm in Illinois. Esther and her husband Carl had two children, Dennis and John.

Esther and Carl worked hard all their lives. They owned and operated a restaurant. Carl died when Esther was 52. Esther continued to work long hours. Esther started a new business, a bowling alley.

By most measures, Esther and Carl were a financial success. They had hundreds of thousands of dollars in the bank. They owned their own home. They even had enough money to invest in some oil wells.

Esther had several grandchildren whom she dearly loved and adored.

At the age of 84, Esther's health started to fail. Fritz, her brother, lived several blocks away. Fritz worked with the local health care workers to provide in house support for some time. It finally reached the point where Esther needed long term care on a full time basis.

Esther sold the house and her memories and moved into an assisted living facility. Three years later, her health continued to fail and Esther had to be moved to a long term care facility.

Like most elderly people, Esther relied on Medicare to pay her health care costs, and had no other insurance to pay for long term care. Esther and her family discovered Medicare does not pay for long term care. All of the costs of assisted living and long term care had to be paid from Esther's hard earned savings. Each month, Fritz withdrew money from her saving accounts.

Esther died when she was 91 years old, spending the last seven years of her life in assisted living and long term care facilities.

When Esther died, there was only enough money to pay for three more months of care. Esther had lived a frugal life in order to provide an inheritance for her children and her grandchildren. Esther would have been devastated had she known all of her hard earned savings went for long term care costs, not her children and grandchildren.

WHAT YOU WILL LEARN IN THIS CHAPTER

According to the Congressional Budget office, the U.S. will spend an estimated $393 billion in 2008 for long term care, not including unpaid services provided by family and friends.

Although nearly half of us will spend the last several years of our lives requiring custodial care, there is no good answer to the question, "How are we going to pay for this?" Unless you have enough assets to cover the costs out of pocket, which can mean a lot of assets for a married couple living in a high cost area, there are only two alternatives: Long Term Care Insurance or Medicaid.

This chapter explains what long term care will cost and who will pay for it.

WHAT WILL LONG TERM CARE COST?

Q. *What does it cost to stay in a long term care facility?*

A. The cost to stay at a long term care facility or a nursing home is very high. In 2010, available data indicates the average annual cost of nursing home care in the U.S. was $75,190. In New York City, the average cost of care was $125,650. In San Francisco, $109,135.

Assuming a 4% inflation rate per year, a New York resident can face long term care costs of $332,000 per year in the year 2025. Two years of care will cost $664,000. Five years of care will cost $1,666,000.

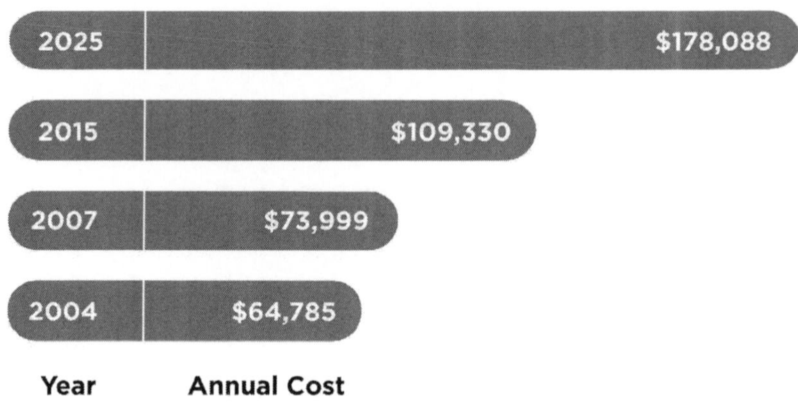

Source: Genworth 2008 Long Term Care Study

WHO PAYS FOR LONG TERM CARE?

Q. *Will Medicare pay for long term care?*

A. Many older people and their children are surprised to find they have no personal insurance to cover the cost of long term care.

When you reach age 65 you can no longer purchase private health insurance as an individual but you become eligible for Medicare, a federally funded health insurance program.

Some people supplement their Medicare benefits through a supplemental health insurance program called Medigap. A variety of Medigap programs are available from private insurance companies.

Medicare and Medigap pay for hospital care, prescriptions and other medical costs. Neither pays for custodial care, i.e., long term care in nursing homes. Medicare does pay for nursing home stays of up to 100 days if you enter the nursing home directly from a hospital, but this is primarily designed to provide post-

surgical nursing, not custodial care.
If the only insurance you have is Medicare and Medigap, the cost of long term care must be paid from your personal assets unless you have Long Term Care Insurance.

Fact: Consumer survey: long term care.

In 2009, a national public opinion research poll showed some 44 percent of Americans incorrectly believed that Medicare or their private health insurance would provide the funding for their long term care needs. Source: Genworth.

Q. *What is long term care insurance?*

A. Long term care insurance policies pay for custodial care, usually in your own home or in a facility. These policies typically cover skilled nursing and other services like therapy, personal care and homemaking. They often have a per day limit, and either a lifetime cap or a time limit. They can be indexed for inflation.

Long term care insurance is expensive. Although the premiums are lower the younger you are, that means that you pay the lower premiums longer. Whether it is really a saving depends on when (or whether) you ever need to make claims under the insurance. But the price of not having long term care coverage may be even more expensive because, if you need care, you will either have to become a burden on some family member or spend down your assets to become eligible for Medicaid.

Fact: Veterans Aid and Attendance benefit program.

If you are a qualified veteran or a spouse of a veteran, a special program called Veterans Aid and Attendance is available to help pay for long term care. **ibutton:** Veterans Aid and Attendance Program www.diesmart.com/ibutton.

Q. *What if you don't have long term care insurance?*

A. A person who has less than $2,000 in assets and income that is insufficient to pay the cost of long term care can apply for financial assistance from Medicaid to help pay for your long term care. If you have assets, you must spend those assets paying for your long term care. After these assets are depleted, you will be poor. Once you are poor, you can apply for financial assistance from Medicaid.

If for some reason you are not eligible for Medicaid, you and your family will continue to be responsible for finding the dollars needed to pay for long term care.

It is unpleasant to think about needing nursing home or home care when you get older. Even more unpleasant is the likelihood that you will have to sacrifice your life's savings to pay for that care. Most unpleasant of all is the likelihood that you may run out of money.

There are ways to mitigate the effect of this on your life and the lives of your heirs. Find a lawyer who specializes in elder care and discuss your options. **ibutton:** Elder Care Lawyers diesmart.com/ibutton

Q. *How can the Class Act help pay for long term care?*

A. The Patient Protection and Affordable Care Act enacted on March 23, 2010, also known as Obama Care, includes language referred to as the Community Living Assistance Services and Support program (CLASS). The Class Act is expected to set up a voluntary government-run long-term care insurance program available through employers. After five years of paying a monthly premium, you'll be covered and can receive benefits if you need care. Watch for more details this year.

WHAT IS MEDICAID?

Q. *How can Medicaid help pay for long term care?*

A. Medicaid is a federal benefit program administered by the states that provides assistance with long term care and nursing home costs to needy people. Medicaid is not insurance. It is a public assistance welfare program funded entirely by taxpayers.

Each state has a department responsible for providing Medicaid benefits to their state residents. Some states have given the state Medicaid program a different name. In California, the Medicaid program is known as Medi-Cal. **ibutton:** State Medicaid Offices www.diesmart.com/ibutton.

info

The original intention of Medicaid was to help provide health care coverage for low-income families. The Medicaid program has morphed into the largest payer of nursing home costs for elderly people who have no money to pay for long term care.

Medicaid is currently paying almost 70% of the costs of long term care provided at nursing homes. Medicaid expenditures were estimated to cost $251 billion in 2009. As 78 million baby boomers age, Medicaid is projected to cost $3.7 trillion between 2008 and 2028.

Q. *How do you qualify for Medicaid assistance?*

A. In order to become eligible for Medicaid you must have very few assets. That means you have to get rid of your assets, either by spending them down or by giving them away. If you give them away, there are penalty periods during which you will not be eligible for Medicaid.

If you are a Medicaid recipient, all social security and pension checks you receive will be applied to the costs of nursing home care. The Medicaid program pays the remaining costs on your behalf to the nursing homes and long term care facilities.

Be aware that Medicaid rules keep changing and that some Medicaid laws differ from state to state. If you are applying for Medicaid, or even just thinking about it, you should consult with an elder care lawyer who is familiar with the Medicaid eligibility and estate recovery rules.

The law also requires individuals applying for or receiving Medicaid to prove their citizenship by submitting a birth certificate or passport.

Q. *Will Medicaid pay for long term care if you own a home?*

A. The Tax Incentive Reduction Act of 2005 states that individuals with more than $500,000 in home equity will be ineligible for Medicaid benefits. States have the option to raise this threshold to $750,000. **ibutton:** State Medicaid home equity rules www.diesmart.com/ibutton.

info

Q. *What happens if the beneficiary you name on your life insurance policy is living in a long term care facility?*

A. If the beneficiary of a life insurance policy is in a long term care facility, the proceeds may become an asset of the beneficiary. These assets will be available to pay the long term care costs of the beneficiary.

If the beneficiary on your life insurance policy enters into a long term care facility, review the existing life insurance beneficiaries. Understand how who you name impacts who pays for your long term care.

WHAT IS THE MEDICAID PENALTY PERIOD?

Q. *What happens if you give some of your assets to your children and then have no funds to pay for your long term care costs?*

A. When you apply for Medicaid, you are required to complete a financial qualifications form. This form asks you to provide an inventory of your financial assets. The form also asks you to list any gifts you have made in the past five years.

The Tax Incentive Reduction Act of 2005 changes how gifts of your assets impact your eligibility to receive Medicaid.

- The law extends the Medicaid "look back" period from three year to five years.

- Most important, the date for removing the value of the gifts from the Medicaid eligibility calculations starts from the day you apply for Medicaid, not the date you made the gift. The look back rule applies to all transfers made on or after February 8, 2006.

If you made gifts within five years before applying for Medicaid, Medicaid will not begin paying for your long term care until the cumulative monthly costs of your care exceed the value of the gifts you made. This period of time when Medicaid is not available is known as the Medicaid Penalty Period.

A Family Story: Medicaid penalty period.

David added his son Eric as a joint tenant on the deed of his personal residence in 2007. At that time, the fair market value of David's house was $100,000. Medicaid will consider Eric's half of the property a gift from David with a value of $50,000.

In May, 2008, David fell and became unable to take care of himself. Eric located a nursing home, but it will cost $5,000 a month. Since David had no assets other than his house, Eric filled out a Medicaid application form requesting help paying for David's nursing home care. David had to list and value the gift of the house on the application form.

David is not eligible for Medicaid benefits for a period of 10 months. The 10-month penalty period was determined by dividing the value of David's gift to Eric ($50K) by the monthly cost of David's long-term care ($5K).

Someone must find the money to pay for David's care the first 10 months. The long term care facility will not accept David as a patient without some means to pay for his care.

WHAT IS THE MEDICAID ESTATE RECOVERY PROGRAM?

Q. *Can Medicaid recover costs it pays on your behalf?*

A. Medicaid rules require you to use your own assets to pay your nursing home costs until they are depleted, at which point Medicaid will help with these costs.

Most state Medicaid programs allow a healthy spouse to continue living in the family home and to keep a small amount of assets if the other spouse needs to be placed in a nursing home. When the healthy spouse dies, the

Medicaid recovery laws allow the state to recover from the proceeds of the sale of the home the costs paid by Medicaid.

Some people think about receiving Medicaid support as similar to obtaining a reverse mortgage on their home. The state, not the bank, pays for their long-term care expenses. You don't need to pay back the loan until the death of the surviving spouse. The state does not charge interest on money it pays for long term care on your behalf.

Q. *Does a state have recourse to collect monies from your estate if you receive Medicaid assistance?*

A. A special debt situation may occur if you are receiving Medicaid when you die. When the Medicaid recipient dies, the state has the right to recover these dollars from your estate. The claims are limited to the amount which Medicaid paid, or the value (fair market value of assets less debt) of the estate assets, whichever is less.

The state is not allowed to pursue the repayment of the Medicaid payments when the recipient dies if:

- A spouse survives the deceased Medicaid beneficiary. The claim to recover the dollars the state spent for the decedent's long term care will be made after the death of the surviving spouse.
- A child under the age of 21 survives the Medicaid beneficiary.
- A child of any age who is blind or disabled (under the Social Security standards) survives the Medicaid beneficiary.

Q. *What type of creditor rights does the state have against your estate?*

A. In many states, Medicaid is simply a creditor and certain other creditors have priority over Medicaid claims. In some states, Medicaid can file under "cost of last illness" and gain priority over other creditors. A federal law passed in 2003 gives states the right to amend their probate laws to make Medicaid a priority creditor. Heirs receive their inheritance only after the Medicaid's priority claims are paid.

A Family Story: Medicaid estate recovery.

Keith designated his son Alex as the beneficiary of the family home, valued at $100,000. At the time of Keith's death, Medicaid had paid $24,000 for his nursing home care. Medicaid filed a creditor claim of $24,000. The estate representative paid back $24,000 to remove the Medicaid lien from the property. Alex inherited $76,000.

Q. *Can Medicaid file a claim against any of your assets?*

A. Under the federal guidelines, states can expand the definition of "estate" to include any property in which an individual had any legal title or interest at the time of death, including assets passed outside probate. A state can define this property to include joint bank accounts, bank accounts with a pay-on-death beneficiary designation, living trusts, life estates in real property, and real estate held in joint tenancy.

Generally, retirement accounts are not subject to estate recovery claims.

If your state uses the expanded definition of "estate", the state has claims against property that would normally not be available for creditor claims.

A Family Story: Expanded state property definition.

After her husband died, Eleanor invited her daughter Sue to come and live with her. Eleanor filed a new deed listing Eleanor and Sue as joint tenants with rights of survivorship.
In the absence of Medicaid claims, Sue as the surviving joint tenant would have automatically inherited the property. Their state has adopted a definition of "estate" that includes all property in which an individual had any legal interest at the time of death.
When Eleanor had to enter a nursing home, Medicaid paid for some of her long term care costs. When Eleanor dies, Medicaid can attach a lien to the property and force Sue to reimburse Medicaid for Eleanor's nursing home care out of what had been Sue's share of the property.

Q. *Can your surviving spouse protect his or her assets after the Medicaid beneficiary dies?*

A. The surviving spouse may limit the amount of his or her estate that will be available for reimbursement of Medicaid expenditures by filing a petition for limitation. The petition must be filed with the state within six months of the death of the Medicaid recipient using forms available from the state. **ibutton:** State Medicaid Offices **www.diesmart.com**/ibutton

info

If a petition is filed, the state will determine the value of the estate of the Medicaid recipient at the time of his or her death. That value will be the limit of the amount available to the state for recovery of its expenditure

WHAT IS THE MEDICAID PARTNERSHIP FOR LONG TERM CARE?

Q. *How can the Medicaid partnership for long term care program help you?*

A. A few states are designing long term care programs providing some type of credit against the cost of insurance premiums back to the policy holder. This arrangement is called the Medicaid Partnership for Long Term Care.

Each state sets its own rules on how the long term care partnership program works. The net impact in these states is that some part of the money you pay for long term care insurance becomes a credit against the lien Medicaid will place against your assets when you die.

The Partnership is an innovative program promoting shared responsibility for financing long term care by linking private long term care insurance to Medicaid. It is a joint effort by state government and private industry to create an option to help you plan to meet your future long term care needs without depleting all of your assets.

The Deficit Reduction Act of 2005 encourages and pushes states to reward citizens who purchase long term care by letting them keep some assets while Medicaid pays for long term care.

Fact: Partnership for Long Term Care program.

The current states offering Partnership for Long Term Care programs are Connecticut, New York, California, Nebraska and Indiana.

Sixteen states are currently looking to provide programs similar to the plan offered in California. **ibutton:** Long Term Care Partnership States www.diesmart.com/ibutton

A Family Story:
Traditional long term care policy versus partnership policy in California.

Arnold and Eunice lived in their home most of their married life. When Arnold's health deteriorated, Arnold moved to a nursing home in San Francisco where he lived the last four years of his life.

Arnold had purchased a long term care policy which paid the first $100,000 of nursing home costs. When long term care insurance was no longer available, Arnold and Eunice did not have enough income to pay for long term care.

Arnold then applied for financial assistance from Medi-Cal. Based upon their assets and income, Arnold qualified for financial assistance from Medi-Cal. Medi-Cal paid an additional $200,000 of long term care costs on behalf of Arnold.

When Arnold died, his estate owed Medi-Cal $200,000.

Arnold's surviving spouse Eunice continued to live in the house until her death. When Eunice died, the Medi-Cal estate recovery program placed a lien on the house.

Their children inherited the house and sold the house for $200,000.

If Arnold had a traditional long term care policy, the entire $200,000 received from the sale of the house would be payable to Medi-Cal. The children would receive no inheritance.

However, if Arnold had purchased a long term care partnership policy, the estate would only owe Medi-Cal $100,000. This is because the terms of a long term care partnership policy treat the long term care costs paid by the policy as a credit against the long term care costs subsequently paid by Medi-Cal. The children would inherit $100,000.

Bottom Line:

You will probably need long term health care insurance. This is almost as certain as death and taxes.

Action Checklist: Plan around Medicare and Medicaid.

- ❑ Find out how much long term care will cost in the state where you live or intend to retire.
- ❑ Determine how you will pay for long term care.
- ❑ Find out if your state offers long term care partnership insurance.
- ❑ Consider buying long term care insurance.
- ❑ Watch for more information about CLASS.
- ❑ Consider the 5-year penalty period and plan accordingly.

Mistake # 3: You did not understand Social Security survivor benefits.

Words to Know:

- Employee Retirement Income Security Act (ERISA)
- Military Survivor Benefit Plan
- Social Security Disability Insurance
- Social Security Retirement Benefits

A Family Story: Two retirement incomes are reduced to one.

Nancy and Jim both had successful careers. Jim is 69 years old. Jim's work record makes Jim eligible to receive a monthly retirement check from Social Security Administration (SSA) in the amount of $1,956. Nancy is 66 years old. Nancy's work record makes Nancy eligible to receive a monthly check from SSA in the amount of $1,700. Their combined monthly SSA retirement income is $3,656.

Jim dies. SSA rules do not allow Nancy to continue receiving two retirement checks. SSA will now only pay one retirement check, which ever is the higher. Since Jim's retirement benefit was higher than Nancy's, SSA will now pay Nancy the monthly benefit previously paid to Jim.

Nancy, the surviving spouse, will find the family social security retirement benefits reduced from $3,656 a month to $1,956 a month.

WHAT YOU WILL LEARN IN THIS CHAPTER

If we are married, we don't know which one of us will die first. What we need to know is when the first spouse dies, what happens to the retirement benefits he or she was receiving.

This chapter explains what happens to retirement benefits when the first spouse dies.

WHAT HAPPENS TO SOCIAL SECURITY BENEFITS?

Q. *What if both spouses are receiving social security retirement checks and one spouse dies?*

A. If you and your surviving spouse both worked and

are both receiving social security retirement benefits, one check stops when the first spouse dies. The surviving spouse is eligible to continue to receive the retirement check paying the higher benefit.

Q. *What happens if the surviving spouse is not caring for minor children and is not at least 62 years of age?*

A. If the surviving spouse is not eligible to receive social security benefits based upon his/her age and work record, the surviving spouse cannot continue to receive the social security retirement check previously being paid to the spouse who died. The surviving spouse must reapply for SSA retirement benefits when he or she meets SSA retirement age qualifications.

A Family Story: Younger wife with no minor or disabled children.

John was 67 when he died. His wife, Mary, was 50 years old. When John died, his social security retirement check of $1,850 stopped. Mary did not meet the age requirements for receiving social security retirement benefits, and had no existing right to John's retirement check. Mary's retirement income went from $1,850 to zero.

When Mary meets the current social security retirement age of 62, she can apply to receive SSA retirement benefits. At that time, SSA will decide whether the benefit would be higher using John's work record or Mary's.

Q. *What happens if the surviving spouse is caring for minor children?*

A. If you are working and paying into Social Security, some of the Social Security taxes you pay go toward survivors insurance.

If the surviving spouse is caring for minor children, he or she is eligible to apply for and receive survivor benefits based upon the work record of the spouse who died.

Q. *Are benefits available for surviving divorced spouses?*

A. A person can receive retirement benefits as a divorced spouse on the decedent's Social Security record if he or she was married to the decedent for at least 10 years, is at least 62 years old, is unmarried and is not entitled to a higher Social Security benefit on his or her own record.

The deceased's former spouse, however, does not have to meet the age or length-of-marriage rule if caring for the decedent's child who is under age 16 or who is disabled.

Survivors benefits paid to a divorced spouse will not affect the benefit rates for other survivors.

Q. *If you were receiving Social Security Disability Insurance (SSDI) checks, do any benefits continue for your survivors?*

A. If the deceased was receiving SSDI benefits, SSDI stops at the time of death because the benefits are based on the needs of the individual and are only paid to the qualifying person.

Although SSDI does not provide survivor benefits, the executor or next of kin should check with the SSA office to see if the surviving spouse or minor children are eligible for other SSA survivor benefits.

WHAT HAPPENS TO PENSIONS PROVIDED BY A FORMER EMPLOYER?

Q. *What happens when the person eligible to receive a pension from a former employer dies?*

A. If your spouse has vested rights to a pension, your rights to a survivor's pension are also vested in the event of his or her death. You will collect a survivor's pension unless you have given a written waiver.

If the deceased spouse is retired and currently receiving pension benefits, the surviving spouse is usually entitled to continue to receive retirement benefits.

Make sure your estate representative knows how to change the name on the retirement account to the surviving spouse.

If the deceased person has not retired, the surviving spouse may still be eligible to receive pension benefits. The surviving spouse should check with the Human Resources department where the deceased worked. At that time, he or she can find out what type of procedure is required to claim survivor benefits.

WHAT HAPPENS TO MILITARY PENSIONS?

Q. *What happens when the retirement check is based upon service in the military?*

A. When a service member starts receiving military retirement benefits, the person serving in the military will be automatically enrolled in an insurance program known as the Survivor Benefit Plan. The insurance premium is automatically deducted from the retirement check and can be set up to pay retirement benefits to a surviving spouse or minor children.

A service member must have written permission from hisor her spouse to not participate in the Survivor Benefit Plan program.

If the survivor benefits insurance is being paid, a surviving spouse, or minor children can continue to receive a portion of the pension.

If the insurance was not purchased, the pension stops upon the death of the person entitled to a military pension.

Fact: Veterans pensions.

Veterans who meet certain net worth and income rules may be eligible for a veteran's pension. In some cases, surviving spouses may also be eligible for a VA pension. Find out more if you or your spouse served at least 90 days in one of the following:

- World War II: December 7, 1941 through December 31, 1946
- Korean War: June 27, 1950 through January 31, 1955
- Vietnam War: August 5, 1964 (February 28, 1961 for veterans who served "in country" before August 5, 1964) through May 7, 1975
- Gulf War: August 2, 1990 through a date to be set by law or presidential proclamation

info

ibutton: Veterans Pension www.diesmart.com/ibutton

Bottom Line:
If you are married, know that when one of you dies your social security benefits will be reduced from two incomes to just one.

Action Checklist: Understand survivor benefits

- ☐ If you are married and both spouses are eligible for social security, create two retirement budget scenarios. One scenario includes the social security benefits of both spouses. The other scenario includes only one retirement check.
- ☐ If you receive retirement benefits from a former employer, make sure someone knows how to transfer benefits to a surviving spouse.
- ☐ If you are receiving a company pension plan, leave instructions on what happens to these benefits when you die.
- ☐ Check eligibility for a veteran's pension.

Mistake # 4: You did not leave a family treasure map

Words to Know:

- Assets
- Digital Assets
- Family Notebook
- Passwords
- Personal Property
- RoboForm
- Safe Deposit Box

A Family Story: What safe deposit box does this key open?

Minna was named as the executor of her father's estate. While going through his belongings, she found a safe deposit box key. However, there were no instructions and no information about where it belonged. Minna spent a week visiting every bank within fifteen miles of where her father lived, all to no avail. Minna still has the safe deposit box key. The missing gold coins may be in the safe deposit box. Minna will never know.

WHAT YOU WILL LEARN IN THIS CHAPTER

A recent article in USA Today stated unclaimed property is now the third largest source of revenue for state government. States are holding $33 billion of unclaimed property. Why? Because someone forgot they owned it or they died without telling someone else they owned it.

Pay attention! Your personal property and your digital assets are not governed by state law and do not have automatic inheritance rights. Unlike your real estate or your bank accounts, there are no default laws defining who inherits this property or has rights to this property. Documenting what you own and what you owe is imperative.

It is equally important to document how to access your electronic financial records or other digital assets. Many of us routinely store personal and financial information on a computer or on a hosted web site. Some of us don't even keep paper records. Unless you tell someone how to access this information, they may not be able to do so.

This chapter explains why it is important to document what you own, what you owe, and where it is.

WHY DO BANKS REPORT MONEY IN YOUR BANK ACCOUNT AS AN UNCLAIMED ASSET?

Q. *What is escheatment?*

A. If you have a safe deposit box or a bank account, the financial institution where the account is held has no legal obligation to locate the owner of the account. In some states, the bank is required by law to send a notice to your last known address, informing you that your account will be transferred to the State Controller for safekeeping if you do not notify the institution of your intent to maintain your account.

If the institution is unable to contact you, or if you fail to contact the institution, the law requires the custodian of your account to remit the account to the state for safekeeping. The State Controller's Office will send a notice informing you of your Unclaimed Property, provided it is able to find a more current address by matching your reported Social Security number with the Franchise Tax Board's records. For example, the State Controller publishes a notice in newspapers of general circulation in each county annually to inform California residents that they may have unclaimed property.

If the notice is sent after your house is sold, or for some reason the post office does not forward the notice to your heirs, your heirs will have no knowledge of these accounts. The state will now own your property. The legal term for this process is escheatment.

How can you make sure this does not happen to you? One of the best gifts you can leave is information about property you own, money you owe, and money owed you. Making a list of what you own and what you owe will be a great help to your estate representative. It is information they need to know but you won't be around to tell them.

WHO HAS RIGHTS TO YOUR DIGITAL ASSETS WHEN YOU DIE?

HOSTED SITES

Q. *How will your spouse or executor gain access to e-mail or other business processes stored on hosted sites?*

A. If you own a small business and your accounting or sales procedures are managed on hosted web sites (for instance Yahoo, Google, eBay, etc.), it is critical someone knows how to access these accounts. Digital assets are considered personal property. There are no default laws determining who has rights to access these assets or statutes an Internet Service Provider (ISP) must follow when someone dies.

The result: each ISP has set their own policies on whether they will provide passwords or user IDs to your spouse, executor or trustee when you die. Some ISPs may not.

If you work in a small business, your chief executive officer or chief financial officer may not be able to access company files without your passwords.

When you set up accounts on hosted services, ask what their policy is regarding user IDs and passwords when someone dies. Plan accordingly. Create and maintain a list of URLs, user IDs and passwords for important data.

Fact: Internet service provider policies.

fyi

AOL. If you have an AOL e-mail account, your executor or trustee can send a letter to AOL requesting your user ID and password, accompanied by a certified copy of your death certificate. AOL will then disclose your user ID and password.

YAHOO. Yahoo will not provide anyone with your user ID and password when you die. Your executor, spouse or business partner will not be able to obtain your user IDs and passwords for any e-mail or other accounting or sales data hosted on their sites.

MSN. If you have an e-mail account with Microsoft, Microsoft will give your executor or spouse access to your address book and instant messaging contacts. They will not disclose your user ID and password. Your e-mail messages can't be read or responded to by anyone who does not know your user ID or password.

ibutton: Internet Service Provider Password Policies
diesmart.com/ibutton

info

YOUR PERSONAL COMPUTER

Q. *How will your employees, executor or spouse gain access to data files stored on your personal computer?*

A. You own the data on your PC. You have the right to leave instructions on who inherits any intellectual property stored on the PC. If you have data you don't want someone to see after you die, be sure to delete it on a scheduled basis. Don't forget to leave any user IDs or passwords someone will need to log on to your computer.

WHO WILL INHERIT AUNT ELEANOR'S PIE PLATE?

Q. What happens to your untitled personal property?

A.. For many families, deciding who will inherit personal property is a big emotional event. Memories are sometimes more important than money. Your heirs are more likely to argue about personal property than

anything else you own.
There are several ways to deal with personal property and keep the peace at the same time. First, you should decide who is going to get what. Just your children? Other close relatives? Friends? You can decide. It's your property, after all.

If you have a will or trust, specify in your will or trust who gets what. Your will or trust should also reference a specific Personal Property Attachment which lists who gets what.

Q. *What is the best way to document your personal property and how you want it divided when you die?*

A. Many products are available to help make a list of your personal property. The information can be completed by hand or stored in electronic records. Most products provide a way to inventory your house room to room and list and photograph personal property in each room. **ibutton:** Family Notebook Reviews www.diesmart.com/ibutton

info

You can provide detailed information such as what it is, where you got it, if it's an heirloom, etc. You can also include who you would like to receive it when you die.

You can also use a digital recorder and make an audio tour of your house, recording items as you walk through each room.

The important thing is that you document what you have, where it is and who gets it when you die. Be aware that simply making a list of your personal property may not be deemed valid and legally enforceable upon your death unless the list is referenced within your will or trust.

WHERE SHOULD YOU STORE YOUR LEGAL DOCUMENTS?

Q. *Where should you store signed originals?*

A. Most people store their legal documents in a fireproof safe at their house or in a safe deposit box. Make sure your executor or your family knows where to find the original and any photocopies of your will, living trust, beneficiary forms, power of attorney, guardianship or other legal documents needed when you die.

You should also provide copies of these documents to a trusted third party in case your documents are destroyed or lost.

Q. *If something happens to the original documents, will a photocopy serve as an authentic document?*

A. Your Last Will and Testament is a unique document. Many states consider only the original signed document as valid because there is no way of knowing whether the original was replaced or merely misplaced.

Some states have procedures for admitting copies of your will to probate after someone submits affidavits swearing that the original was not replaced. For this reason, the attorney who drafted the will frequently keeps the original. Make sure someone knows the location of your original will.

Photocopies of other legal documents, including your living will, living trust and power of attorney, can be treated as an authentic document. Some states require a notary signature on the photocopy of the form.

Q. *Can you store electronic copies of your legal documents?*

A. The only document that needs to be an original is a will. (Arizona is unique; there, you can store an electronic copy of a will.) Other documents can be stored electronically in several states

---

Fact:
Electronic storage.

If you live in Arizona, you can store an electronic copy of your will. Arizona law gives the electronic will the same validity as an original printed signed will.

Other states provide electronic living will registries, including Wisconsin, Montana, Nevada, Wyoming, Washington, Louisiana, and North Carolina.

ibutton: Living Will Registry States diesmart.com/ibutton

Q. *What is involved in accessing a will or living trust kept in a safe deposit box?*

A. If these documents are stored in a safe deposit box, state law will determine who has the right to access them.

- If the safe deposit box is owned by the trust, the successor trustee automatically has the right to access the box.
- If you owned the box as an individual or as joint tenants, access for your successor may not always

be immediate. Some states require a copy of the death certificate before they grant access to the box.

info **ibutton:** State Safe Deposit Rules www.diesmart.com/ibutton

Q. *Does the person who accesses your safe deposit box own the contents of the safe deposit box?*

A. No. Just because someone has access to the safe deposit box doesn't mean they have inheritance rights to the stored items. Some states require the bank officer to take an inventory when the estate representative requests access to the box. We recommend you keep an inventory of items kept in the safe deposit box.

Q. *If you change the name on your checking account to the trust, does this also change the name on your safe deposit box?*

A. No. Some banks may not automatically change the name on your safe deposit box to the trust when you change the name on your checking account.

If you have a living trust and are transferring title of your checking account from an individual account to a trust account, make sure you also complete the necessary form to change the name on your safe deposit box from you as an individual to you as trustee of your living trust.

Make sure you get a copy of a document showing that the trust owns the box and file a copy of the ownership documents with your estate planning files.

Bottom Line:

$

Just like "x marks the spot," create a treasure map for your survivors. Let them know where everything is and how to get access to it. If they can't ask you, how will they know?

Action Checklist: Create a Family Treasure Map

- ❑ Set up an estate filing system. Make it easy for your children or surviving spouse to find documents and other records they will need.

- ❑ Obtain certified copies of your birth, marriage or divorce papers. Someone will need these documents to manage your financial affairs.

- ❑ Create a personal property schedule. Talk with your children about any special desires they may have. Determine an equitable way to distribute your personal property.

- ❑ Understand who has the rights to your safe deposit box.

- ❑ Use RoboForm to store and record passwords and user IDs for on-line accounts. Make sure someone knows any administration codes or user IDs needed to access your personal computer or files on your computer.
  ibutton: Roboform diesmart.com/ibutton

info

- ❑ Sit down with your executor and your family. Make sure they know how to locate your property. If you keep your records on the Internet, or on a computer, make sure someone knows how to access your electronic records.

Mistake # 5: You thought living trusts were just for rich people

Words to Know:

- Beneficiary
- Grantor
- Probate
- Revocable Living Trust
- Settlor
- Successor Trustee
- Testamentary Trust
- Trustee

A Family Story: Property control

Luther's wife died three years ago. Luther has two adult children. Luther meets Josephine, a widower who also has two adult children.

Josephine and Luther marry and decide to combine their assets. They complete new documents identifying Luther and Josephine as joint tenants with the right of survivorship on their checking accounts, their brokerage accounts, and the deeds to both of their houses.

One year later, Luther dies. Josephine, the surviving joint tenant, now owns her share and Luther's share of the property. When Josephine dies, Josephine's will or trust determines who inherits the property. If Josephine does not have a will or trust, the state intestate laws of succession determine who inherits the property.

In some states, the laws of succession do not give stepchildren any inheritance rights. Unless Josephine names Luther's children as beneficiaries in her will or trust, Luther's children will inherit none of Luther's share of the assets.

WHAT YOU WILL LEARN IN THIS CHAPTER

In the movies we watch or the books we read, the wealthy are visiting their bankers to talk about their trusts. Our high school and college textbooks only discuss wills. It's no wonder many of us think trusts are just for the wealthy.

The fact is trusts are not just for the wealthy. Many people are using trusts as a fundamental planning tool because trusts give them and their successors more flexibility to manage their assets before and after death. A living trust can also allow someone of modest means to avoid the cost and delays of probate.

Trusts can be created while you are living or created after you die according to the instructions you provide in your will. A common trust created while you are living is referred to as a revocable living trust. A trust created after you die based upon instructions you provide in your will is known as a testamentary trust.

There are many types of trusts. Our discussion focuses on the use of living trusts and testamentary trusts.

This chapter explains what a trust is, how a trust differs from a will and what happens if you die without a will or a living trust.

WHAT IS A TRUST?

Q. *How do you create a trust?*

A. A trust is an agreement creating a legal entity that can own property. Trust agreements are private documents. They are generally not filed with a court or other public entity.

There is no specific form used to create a trust. In general, a trust is made when:

- The trust document is signed by the person making the trust, called "the Settlor"; and
- the trustee changes the title on property being held as an individual to a title held in the name of the trustee.

Once the trust is made, the agreement may be amended and/or revoked, usually only by the person who originated the trust, e.g., the Settlor.

The trust agreement specifies:

- The person who is in charge of managing the trust assets. This person is called the trustee. If a married couple creates a trust, they may be co-trustees.
- The duties and powers of the trustee relating to how certain assets are to be held and managed. Once

assets are titled in the name of the trustee, the trustee may then manage the assets based on the powers described in the trust agreement.

- The beneficiaries and the conditions on which the trustee is to distribute certain assets and certain parts of assets (i.e. income and principal).

- The name of the successor trustee. The successor trustee has the legal authority to take control of trust assets when the original trustee or co-trustees die or become incapacitated.

WHAT IS THE DIFFERENCE BETWEEN A LIVING TRUST AND A TESTAMENTARY TRUST?

Q. *What is a revocable living trust?*

A. A revocable living trust is a trust you create while you are living. It is a revocable trust because its terms can be revoked and/or amended until you become incapacitated or die. The living trust document (a) describes how you want your trust assets to be managed during your lifetime and after your death and (b) names one or more trustee(s) to manage trust assets according to the instructions specified in the trust agreement.

It is common for you, the person who makes the trust, to name yourself as the initial trustee. If a husband and wife create the trust, it is common that both Settlors are named as the initial co-trustees.

The trust has the legal right to own property. Once a trust is created, the individual who created the trust can transfer the title of property owned as an individual to the name of the trust. At the time of the Settlor's death, his or her property is titled in the name of the trustee, rather than in the Settlor's name as an individual. Because an individual does not own the property, property owned by a trust is not subject to probate.

Q. *What is a testamentary trust?*

A. A testamentary trust is a trust described in a will, created upon the death of the decedent. The trust agreement is actually embedded in the text of the will. In such a case, the trust did not exist at the time of the death of the decedent. It only was created following death. As a result, the trust is funded with probate assets.

The testamentary trust can provide some of the same features as a living trust: directions for managing assets for minor children, directing and providing income for your spouse or children, and providing ongoing control of trust property. It cannot, however, be used as a method of avoiding probate because assets are not transferred to the trust until after you die. As the property is owned by you as an individual until your death, property is transferred to the testamentary trust after you die.

WHAT IS THE DIFFERENCE BETWEEN A WILL AND A TRUST?

Trusts offer certain features not available in a will. Living trusts offer certain features not available in a testamentary trust.

CONTROL OF ASSETS AFTER YOU DIE

A Will	A Trust
A will generally describes who inherits certain assets after your death.	Your trust can include instructions giving someone the right to income and the use of the property during their lifetime.
If you leave property outright to someone in a will, they become the owners of the property at the conclusion of probate.	When these beneficiaries die, your trust can include irrevocable instructions on who has the right to income and the use of the property.
When your beneficiary dies, their will, or state intestate succession rules, determine who will inherit the property you gave them, assuming they have not transferred or sold it prior to that time.	There are many situations in which you may want to control the second instance of inheritance. For example:
	• You want to provide your children with income but you want the assets to go to your grandchildren. • You have been married before. You want to provide income for your surviving spouse but also want to be sure your children from your prior marriage inherit some portion of your assets when your surviving spouse dies. • You want to be sure your children inherit your separate assets if you die first, eliminating any opportunity for a spouse or stepchildren to claim rights to your separate property. • You have minor or disabled children and you want to provide for their support and choose when (or if) they inherit the principal.
The intended time frame of probate is actually as short as possible—the process is not intended to allow an executor to spend years managing the assets in the estate.	A trust agreement may include elaborate directions regarding the management of certain trust assets and may contemplate an administration that lasts a very long time.
The executor may not be able to take control of probate assets without approval of the court, which may take some period of time.	A trustee can take immediate control of trust assets.

A Family Story: Second marriage property control.

Brad and Heather had been married for twenty years. It was Brad's second marriage. His children from a prior marriage had been living with Brad and Heather since they were babies. Brad knew Heather would take care of his children if he died first.

Brad died in a hunting accident. His will gave everything he owned to Heather. Heather died six months later. Heather had no will and died intestate. The state intestate laws had no provision for giving assets to stepchildren. All of Heather's assets (which now included Brad's) went to Heather's parents. Brad's children inherited nothing.

MANAGEMENT OF MONEY FOR MINOR CHILDREN

A Will	A Trust
If you leave money to your minor children via your will, a guardian or custodian will need to be appointed by the court to manage the funds.	If you leave money to your minor children via your trust, your trustee will manage the trust assets for the benefit of your minor children according to the instructions you include in the trust.
Depending upon the size of the inheritance, the courts may even govern how the money ought to be invested.	These instructions can include the age at which you want your child to have access and control of the funds. For instance, you can give a child access to 1/3 of their inheritance at age 25, 1/3 at age 30 and 1/3 at age 35.
When the child becomes an adult, at age 18 or 21 depending upon state law, he or she becomes the owner of all of the assets.	

CREDITOR NOTIFICATION

A Will	A Trust
If you have a will and your assets are subject to probate, a formal creditor notification process must occur before the court approves completion of the probate.	If you have a trust, the trustee procedures in many states do not include formal creditor notification or creditor release processes.
The creditor must respond with any claims against the estate.	There may be no time limit on when a creditor may file a claim.
Once the time for filing a claim has expired, the estate is not subject to future claims from the creditor.	Some states, including California, allow a trustee to use the same creditor notification process available with a will.

CHILDREN WITH SPECIAL NEEDS

A Will	A Trust
If you give assets to a special needs child via a will, the assets are now considered property owned by the child. The value of the assets may eliminate the opportunity for a child with special needs to obtain assistance from available local, state or federal assistance programs.	If your trust has instructions to manage assets on behalf of a special needs child, these assets are not considered to be owned by the special needs child. As such, the value of these assets is not considered when applying for local, state or federal assistance.

THE USE OF A TRUST MAY HELP YOU AVOID PROBATE IN MULTIPLE STATES

A Will	Only A Living Trust
Assets you own as an individual or that are owned by your estate are subject to probate.	If you transfer the title of property you own as an individual to your living trust, the trustee is the owner of the property.
If you own real estate in more than one state, your estate representative may need to open a probate case in multiple states.	Trust assets are generally not subject to probate in any state.

A Will	Only A Living Trust
All documents filed with the courts are public information.	Your private life usually remains private.
Court fees and legal fees are set by state statute.	Your legal fees are negotiated or set by you, not set by statute.
The estate representative does not have immediate access to probate assets. For example, if the stock market is falling, the estate representative may have to wait for and/or seek approval from the courts to buy or sell stocks.	Your estate representative has immediate access to your assets. If the stock market is falling, he or she can take immediate corrective action.
	A testamentary trust does not avoid the need for probate, as the property is not transferred to the trust before your death. The probate courts will oversee the creation, funding and administration of your testamentary trust.

AUTHENTIC DOCUMENT

A Will	Only A Living Trust
If you have a will, most states require your estate representative to file the original document. If the original document cannot be found, some states will consider you to have died intestate.	If you have a trust, copies of your living trust are considered authentic, binding documents.

CONSERVATOR ALTERNATIVE

A Will	Only A Living Trust
If you have a will and become incapacitated, nothing in your will can help manage your assets while you are living.	If you have a trust, your co-trustee or successor trustee can continue to manage trust assets without a court supervised guardianship. Court supervised guardianships cost money and require the courts to supervise how someone manages your assets. A testamentary trust is created after you die. It does not provide value if you become incapacitated.

A Family Story: Living Trust avoids conservatorship.

Robert and Linda decided to retire after selling their business. They met with an estate planning lawyer. Robert and Linda lived in California, a state where probate fees are based upon the gross value of your estate. Robert and Linda also had a vacation home in Arizona, titled as joint tenants with right of survivorship.

Their attorney recommended they create a living trust and transfer the title of their real estate to the trust, eliminating the need for probate in both California and Arizona.

He also included language in the trust giving Robert and Linda the right to manage trust assets for each other in case one became incapacitated.

Robert and Linda created and signed their living trust and named each other as trustees. They named Robert's brother, John, as the successor trustee.

Robert and Linda completed new deeds naming Robert and Linda, trustees of the Robert and Linda trust as the owners. They also changed the ownership documents on their bank accounts, their brokerage accounts and their vehicles.

Robert and Linda completed a personal property schedule, listing the art they owned and the individuals they wanted to inherit the art when they died.

Robert and Linda funded their trust. They no longer owned their property as individuals. The probate courts no longer had the responsibility to manage these assets since an individual didn't own the property.

A year after retiring, Linda was diagnosed with Alzheimer's disease. Robert had two doctors examine Linda. Both issued statements stating Linda was unable to make decisions for herself. Robert continued to have the authority to manage assets owned by the trust. There was no need for the probate courts to be involved in any incompetency or conservatorship hearings.

Two years later, Robert died. John, as successor trustee, follows the instructions in the trust and will continue to manage the trust assets on behalf of Linda. Property owned by a trust is not subject to probate.

Setting up a trust eliminated the fees and public nature of probate for Robert and Linda.

ESTATE TAX PLANNING FOR MARRIED COUPLES

A Will	A Trust
If a surviving spouse files Form 706 on time and claims a Deceased Spouse Unused Exclusion Amount, a married couple can exclude up to $10 million from the federal estate tax..	If you have a trust, the trust instructions can set up new trusts when you die, sometimes referred to as A/B trusts.
If you are married and do not file Form 706 on time when the first spouse dies, a surviving spouse can only use his or her $5 million exemption allowance.	The use of the A/B trust enables both you and your surviving spouse to claim their federal estate tax exemption allowance, potentially saving the estate millions of dollars. See Mistake #6 for more information about A/B trusts.

ACCESS TO SAFE DEPOSIT BOX

A Will	Only A Living Trust
If you own your safe deposit box as an individual or as the last surviving joint tenant, upon your death your estate representative must follow state rules on how and when the safe deposit box may be accessed.	If your trust owns a safe deposit box, the trustee is considered the owner and has the legal right to access the box at any time. A testamentary trust cannot "own" a safe deposit box because a testamentary trust is not created until after you die.

COST TO CREATE VERSUS COST OF PROBATE

A Will	Only A Living Trust
If you visit a lawyer, you will find it usually costs more to create a living trust than a will.	If you die with a will, the costs of probate or a conservatorship may offset the cost to create the living trust. A testamentary trust does not avoid probate.

A Family Story: The high cost of probate.

Joe's father Paul was having difficulty walking. Joe recommended his father purchase an automated wheel chair and a van equipped for wheel chair access.

Two months later, Paul died. Although Paul had a living trust established several years before his death, the van title and registration documents listed Paul as the owner. Because Paul owned the van as an individual, the van was a probate asset.

Joe discovered he needed documents from the probate court giving him the legal authority to sell the van. Joe hired a lawyer and filed documents with the probate court requesting the court grant him the authority he needed.

The value of the used van and the wheel chair was $25,000. The legal and court costs required to get approval from the probate court to sell the vehicle and wheel chair were $9,000.

MANAGEMENT OF A BUSINESS

Your Will	Only A Living Trust
If you have an ownership interest in a business, the ownership interest will likely be part of your probate estate if your estate plan is based on a will or you don't have any estate planning documents.	If you have placed your ownership interest in a trust, the trustee may manage your portion of the business interest without the need for court intervention or court costs. A testamentary trust will not avoid probate as your ownership in your business was not transferred to your trust before you died.

HOW DOES A TRUST WORK?

Q. *Who manages the trust assets while you are living and when you die?*

A. The person originally making the trust selects and names the trustee and the successor trustee. The trustee can be a financial institution, or it can be an individual.

The person who originally makes a trust, the "Settlor", usually names himself or herself as the initial trustee of the trust, and identify other people in whom he or she has confidence to serve as the successor trustee(s).

If you name yourself as the trustee when you create the trust, you manage the trust assets while you are living.

When the original trustee can no longer act because of death, resignation or incapacity, the successor trustee you named will now manage the trust assets according to the instructions and rules described in the trust agreement.

Selecting a successor trustee is an important decision. Many people select an adult child and often such a choice is a solid one. However, you should consider the effect such a decision will have on any other siblings and whether any tension between the siblings may affect the administration of the trust.

Fact: Trustee fees.

A trustee is generally paid "a reasonable fee". When "institutional trustees" are named (such as a trust division of a bank), such institutions will charge a management fee to manage the trust assets, usually 1 to 2 percent of the value of the trust assets.

HOW DOES THE TRUSTEE TRANSFER ASSETS TO THE TRUST?

Q. *How does property with a title become a trust asset?*

A. Without a trust, assets you own can be titled in your name as an individual or as a joint tenant. Once you establish a trust, you can also title property in the name of the trustee.

To place assets in trust, the assets should be titled in the name of the person identified as trustee of the trust. For instance, your house title may list the owners as John and Mary Jones. Once the trust is created, you would file the necessary paperwork to change the title to John and Mary Jones, trustees for the John and Mary Jones Trust.

The trustee should create the paperwork necessary to change title on bank accounts, brokerage accounts, real property and other titled assets transferred to the trust.

Talk with a professional before deciding what assets to put in the trust.

Q. *How does property without a title become a trust asset?*

A. Much of the property we own does not have a title, including our jewelry, art, collectibles and household items. You should prepare a Trust Schedule itemizing the property you want to be managed as a trust asset. Make sure the trust documents refer to the Trust Schedule.

Q. *What if you don't title property in the name of the trustee or create a Trust Schedule?*

A. If the title is still held in the name of an individual, these assets are not trust assets. When you die, these assets will be managed as either a probate asset or an automatic inheritance asset.

Fact: IRAs and Living Trusts.

The IRS may view the transfer of your retirement accounts to a trust as a withdrawal. You will need to report the withdrawal on your tax return and pay any taxes due.

Do not transfer your IRA to your living trust before talking with an IRA expert.

HOW DOES A LIVING TRUST IMPACT YOUR TAXES?

Q. *If you have living trust, how does it impact your income tax returns?*

A. For IRS purposes, doing business as a trustee is the same as doing business as an individual. You will report any income or expenses related to assets owned by your living trust in the same manner you would as if they were owned by you as an individual.

- You don't need a separate tax identification number for the trust while you are living.
- You can still deduct mortgage payments.
- You use the same rules for calculating gains and losses when you buy or sell trust assets.

Q. *If you have trust assets, how do they impact your estate taxes?*

A. They don't. Trust assets are considered part of your taxable estate when you die. Trust assets are subject to estate taxes in the same manner as if they were owned by an individual.

WHY DO YOU NEED BOTH A LIVING TRUST AND A WILL?

Q. *If you have a living trust, why do you need a will?*

A. There are several reasons.

First, it is almost certain that when you die you will have assets which you have not transferred into the name of the trustee of the trust. You need a way to deal with those assets, even if all you do is write a will that pours them over into the trust.

This type of will is referred to as a "Pour Over Will." The instructions in a pour over will usually center around a single specific bequest, giving all of the estate assets to the trustee of the trust, so these assets may be administered under the terms of the trust.

Second, if you are leaving estate assets for the benefit of a minor child, in some states you may need a will to nominate a guardian of the person for the minor and/or disabled child for whom you are leaving the gift.

WHAT IF YOU DIE WITHOUT A WILL OR A LIVING TRUST?

Q. *What if you don't make a will or a living trust?*

A. If you don't make a will or a trust, you are considered to have died intestate. Upon your death the following will occur:

- Property with automatic inheritance rights will automatically be transferred to the named beneficiaries.
- The remaining property will be distributed according to the applicable state laws of intestacy. These are laws which describe who inherits your probate property when you fail to leave a will.
- An estate representative, sometimes called an administrator or a personal representative, will be appointed by the court to administer your intestate estate. Most state laws contain a preference that a surviving spouse, and then surviving children, be appointed to serve as the administrator of the intestate estate.
- The court appointed estate representative has the same responsibility as someone you appoint as an executor in your will or the successor trustee in your living trust, except they are not guided by a will or a trust. Their actions are governed by state laws only. Under most state laws of intestacy, the probate assets are divided among a surviving spouse and children of the decedent. However, if there is no surviving spouse and no surviving children, then the intestate assets are distributed to next of kin. In most states, stepchildren have no right to inherit. If there are no surviving relatives, the entire probate estate may go to the state. **ibutton:** State Intestate Succession Statutes www.diesmart.com/ibutton

Bottom Line:

$

Consult an attorney. Explain your family situation. Decide whether to create either a trust or a will, or both.

Action Checklist:

Compare the advantages of a living trust with a will for you and your family.

- ❑ If you have children from a prior marriage, ask your lawyer how your estate plan will protect their inheritance if you die first.

- ❑ If you have minor children, ask your lawyer how you can specify at what age your children may receive their inheritance.
- ❑ Compare the cost of probate in your state to the cost of creating a living trust.
- ❑ Ask how long it will take for your children to receive their inheritance if probate is required or if the assets are owned by a trust.
- ❑ Choose your executor and trustee wisely. They need to be family diplomats and be able to understand complex legal and financial rules.

Mistake #6: You did not understand the married couple estate tax trap

Words to Know:

- Deceased Spouse Unused Exclusion Amount (DSUEA)
- A/B Trust
- Estate Tax
- Federal Estate Tax Personal Exemption
- Gift Tax
- Irrevocable Trust
- State Inheritance Tax
- Taxable Estate

A Family Story:
First spouse unintentionally gives millions of dollars to the government.

Marilyn and George had been married for fifty years.

The 2010 Tax Relief Act gives each person the right to exclude $5 million of taxable assets from the federal estate tax. The Act also gives a surviving spouse the ability to claim and preserve the unused portion of the first spouse to die $5 million exclusion amount.

George died in March, 2011. George's taxable estate was $4 million, which George left to Marilyn, his surviving spouse. The marital deduction law excludes these assets from any federal estate tax.

Marilyn died in November, 2012. Marilyn's estate now includes assets Marilyn owns and assets Marilyn inherited from George. Marilyn's estate is valued at $9 million.

Jane, the daughter and executor discovered Marilyn had made a million dollar mistake when George died. Marilyn had not completed and filed a Form 706 estate tax return with the Internal Revenue Service.

Because the Form 706 estate tax return was not filed when George died, Marilyn's estate lost the right to use George's deceased spouse unused exclusion amount of $5 million.

Marilyn's estate had to pay $1,380,000 in federal estate taxes.

When George died:		
George's taxable estate		$4,000,000
George's 2011 exemption allowance	-$5,000,000	
Estate subject to federal tax (Unlimited Marital Deduction)		-$0
George's Deceased Spouse Unused Exclusion Amount		$0
When Marilyn died:		
Marilyn's taxable estate		$9,000,000
Marilyn's 2012 exemption allowance	-$5,000,000	
George's Deceased Spouse Unused Exclusion Amount	$0	
Total estate excluded from estate tax		-$5,000,000
Estate subject to estate tax		$4,000,000
Estate taxes due		$1,380,000
Jane inherits		$7,620,000

Marilyn's estate cannot use George's unused $5 million exclusion amount because no one filed Form 706 when George died. Marilyn's estate can only exclude $5 million of taxable assets from the federal estate tax.

Marilyn unintentionally gave the government George's unused $5 million exemption allowance. Jane inherits $7,620,000.

Same Family Story: Form 706 filed on time.

When George died, Marilyn filed Form 706 with the IRS and claimed a $5 million deceased spouse unused exclusion amount.

When George Died		
George's taxable estate		$4,000,000
George's 2011 exclusion amount	-$5,000,000	
Estate subject to federal tax (Unlimited Marital Deduction)		-$0
George's Deceased Spouse Unused Exclusion Amount		$5,000,000
When Marilyn Died		
Marilyn's taxable estate		$9,000,000
Marilyn's 2012 exemption allowance	-$5,000,000	
George's Deceased Spouse Unused Exclusion Amount	-$5,000,000	
Total Amount excluded from estate tax		-$10,000,000
Estate subject to estate taxes		$0
Estate taxes due		$0
Jane Inherits		$9,000,000

Marilyn's estate can combine Marilyn's $5 million personal exemption allowance with George's $5 million deceased spouse unused exclusion amount. Together, Marilyn and George can exclude $10 million of assets from the federal estate tax.

Marilyn took advantage of the 2010 Tax Act portability law. Marilyn's estate owed no federal estate taxes. Jane inherits $9,000,000.

WHAT YOU WILL LEARN IN THIS CHAPTER

Benjamin Franklin once said, "In this world nothing is certain but death and taxes." Boy was he right. When you die, a special tax known as the federal estate tax comes into effect.

Throughout our nation's history, death and estate taxes have been imposed many times by Congress. The first death "stamp" tax was levied by the federal government for a period of five years in 1797. It was re-enacted from 1862 to 1870 to help pay for the Civil War and again in 1898 thru 1902 to help pay for the Spanish American War.

The present system of federal estate taxes was established in 1916 and amended several times thereafter.

It's difficult to explain the current laws regarding estate and gift taxes because our existing estate tax laws are only temporary laws.

In 2001, Congress passed the first temporary estate tax law, referred to as the Economic Growth and Tax Relief Act ("EGTRRA"). This act established the estate and gift tax laws for someone who dies between January 1, 2002 and December 31, 2010.

In December, 2010, Congress passed a second temporary estate tax law, referred to as the Tax Relief, Unemployment Insurance Reauthorization, and Job Creation Act of 2010 (TRA2010). This act established the estate and gift tax laws for someone who dies between January 1, 2010 and December 31, 2012.

If someone dies in the year 2010, the estate is governed by both the 2001 tax relief act and the 2010 tax relief act. An executor or trustee can elect whether the estate will be subject to the 2001 EGTRRA laws or the 2010 Tax Relief Act laws.

Currently, someone who dies after December 31, 2012, will be subject to the estate and gift tax laws in place before the temporary laws were passed in 2001.

Federal and state estate tax systems are complex and at the moment, temporary. For those with sizeable assets or complex personal relationships it is a good idea to consult with a certified public accountant or an estate planning lawyer. They can help you plan based upon the rules for dying in the year 2011 or 2012. At this time, it is uncertain what the laws will be for someone who dies on or after January 1, 2013.

The discussion in this chapter describes the estate tax laws prescribed in the 2010 Tax Relief Act and are applicable for the years 2011 or 2012. Some part of these laws would also be applicable to someone who dies in the year 2010 if the estate representative elected to use the estate tax laws contained in the 2010 Tax Relief Act.

If someone dies in the year 2010, the estate representative can choose to use the estate tax laws defined in the 2001 EGTRAA or the 2010 Tax Relief Act. Find out more at www.diesmart.com.

info

This chapter explains what the federal estate tax is, how to calculate the value of your taxable estate, and several ways you can minimize estate taxes.

WHAT IS THE FEDERAL ESTATE TAX?

Q. *Who is subject to paying the federal estate tax?*

A. The federal estate tax is a tax levied when the taxable value of all of your assets is in excess of your personal estate tax exemption allowance. Federal tax laws allow you to transfer a certain amount of assets tax-free when you die. The tax-free amount is referred to as your personal estate tax exemption allowance.

Estate taxes are generally federal taxes and are applicable to everyone; they are a debt of your estate. The estate representative pays the estate taxes before distributing assets to the beneficiaries.

Some states have estate or inheritance taxes as well.

WHAT ASSETS ARE PART OF YOUR TAXABLE ESTATE?

Q. *What assets are subject to the estate tax?*

A. All of your assets are subject to the federal estate tax calculation. Assets include real estate, bank accounts, cash, motor vehicles, stocks, bonds and other securities, jewelry, fine arts or furniture, notes receivable, stock options, deferred compensation, IRAs, Keoghs, retirement plans, pensions, 401(k) plans, life insurance proceeds and all interests in businesses and business property including shares in partnerships, joint ventures, farms, rights to royalties, value of intellectual property, etc.

The gross value of the estate also includes the value of any gifts given away within two years of your death that exceeded the annual gift tax allowance, currently $13,000 per person.

Q. *Are assets with a named beneficiary part of your taxable estate?*

A. Yes. The probate value of your estate and the estate tax value of your estate are separate calculations. When deciding if your estate is subject to the federal estate tax, all of your property, including retirement accounts and life insurance proceeds with a named beneficiary, are included as part of your estate property.

HOW DO YOU CALCULATE THE TAXABLE VALUE OF YOUR ESTATE?

Q. *How is the taxable value of your estate calculated?*

A. Your estate representative must make a list of property you own and, perhaps with the help of an appraiser, assign a fair market value to the property.

The fair market value is the amount the property is worth at the time you die (or six months later if the value is lower than at date of death), not the price you paid for it. Then, he or she must make a list of all the debts you owed at your death.

If you own property jointly with someone else, multiply your ownership share times the fair market value to calculate the estate tax value of the property.

The taxable value of your estate is calculated by deducting the total amount of your debts from the total fair market value of all your assets.

If the taxable value of your estate exceeds the personal estate tax exemption allowance, your executor must file a Form 706 Federal Estate tax return and pay the appropriate tax due within nine months of your death.

- The amount of tax due is calculated by multiplying the estate tax rate applicable the year you die by the value of your net taxable estate.

A probate case cannot be closed until evidence is presented to the court that any estate taxes owed by your estate have been paid. Some banks will not release accounts to the beneficiary until estate taxes are paid.

WHAT IS THE PERSONAL ESTATE TAX EXEMPTION ALLOWANCE?

Q. *How do you determine the amount of your personal federal estate tax exemption?*

A. The personal tax exemption allowance for someone who dies in the year 2011 or 2012 is $5 million. This means no federal estate taxes are due unless the taxable value of your estate exceeds $5 million.

With the proper use of the deceased spouse unused exclusion amount, a married couple can exclude $10 million of their taxable estate from the federal estate tax.

Unless Congress passes a new permanent estate tax law or extends our existing temporary estate tax laws, the estate tax laws revert back to the year 2001.

- The personal estate tax exemption allowance is $1 million. The maximum tax rate is 55%.

- There is no portability of the first spouse to die marital exemption allowance to a surviving spouse. A married couple MUST set up an A/B trust in order to preserve the exemption allowance of the first spouse to die.

The table below lists the Personal Exemption Allowance in place for someone who dies in the years 2001 through 2013. The table also indicates how married couples can preserve the exemption allowance of the first spouse to die.

Federal Estate Tax by Year of Death
Exemption Allowance and Spousal Portability Option

Year	Personal Tax Exemption: Tax-Free Amount	Spousal Portability
2001	$1,000,000	A/B Trust
2002	$1,500,000	A/B Trust
2003	$1,500,000	A/B Trust
2004	$1,500,000	A/B Trust
2005	$2,000,000	A/B Trust
2006	$2,000,000	A/B Trust
2007	$2,000,000	A/B Trust
2008	$2,000,000	A/B Trust
2009	$3,500,000	A/B Trust
2010 - 2010 Tax Relief Act OR	$5,000,000	DSUEA
2010 - 2001 EGTRRA Act	No Tax	A/B Trust
2011	$5,000,000	DSUEA
2012	$5,000,000	DSUEA
2013 and all years thereafter	$1,000,000	A/B Trust

Fact: Only a few pay estate taxes.

The current personal exemption allowance is $5 million. With the proper paperwork, married couples can exclude $10 million of assets from the federal estate tax. At the present time, only a few pay federal estate taxes.

WHAT IS PORTABILITY OF THE DECEASED SPOUSE UNUSED EXCLUSION AMOUNT (DSUEA)?

Q. *Why is the DSUEA important for married couples?*

A. Before the Tax Relief Act of 2010, the only way a married couple could preserve the estate tax exemption allowance of the first spouse to die was to spend time and money in setting up an A/B trust before the first spouse died.

The 2010 Tax Relief Act gives a surviving spouse the right to preserve the deceased spouse unused exclusion amount by the timely filing of Form 706 with the Internal Revenue Service. The surviving spouse can then claim and use the deceased spouse unused exclusion amount even if the first spouse to die has no will or trust.

The ability to transfer the unused estate tax exemption allowance of the first spouse to die to the surviving spouse is sometimes referred to as "portability".

Portability gives married couples the right to exclude $10 million of their taxable estate from federal estate taxes.

Here's an example of how portability can work for John and Mary, a married couple:

- John dies in 2011. John's estate is valued at $5 million.
- John leaves all of his assets to Mary, his wife. The marital deduction law excludes these assets from any federal estate tax.
- John's estate files a timely Form 706 estate tax return with the IRS and claim John's unused $5 million exclusion amount.
- Mary dies in 2012. Mary's estate can claim and exclude $10 million of assets from estate taxes by combining Mary's $5 million exemption allowance with John's $5 million DSUEA.

> If John had left $1 million of his estate to his children and $4 million to Mary, the estate would have filed for a $4 million DSUEA.
>
> If John had left $5 million of his estate to his children, the surviving spouse could not claim any deceased spouse unused exclusion amount.

Q. *Is portability automatic?*

A. No. The surviving spouse or someone settling the estate of the first spouse to die must file Form 706 in a timely manner to claim and document the unused exclusion amount, even if no estate taxes are due. Unless Form 706 is filed, the estate of the surviving spouse loses the ability to use the unused exclusion amount of the first spouse to die.

Q. *What happens if the surviving spouse remarries?*

A. If the surviving spouse remarries, the estate of the surviving spouse must use the deceased spouse unused exclusion amount of the last spouse.

Here is an example:

- When John, Mary's first husband died, Mary filed for a $5 million DSUEA.
- Mary then marries Jim.
- Jim dies in 2012 and leaves his $4 million estate to children from his first marriage.
- Mary must file a new Form 706 in a timely manner and claim a $1 million deceased spouse unused exclusion amount. The $5 million DSUEA Mary had filed for John, her first husband, is no longer available to Mary.
- If Mary dies in 2012, her estate can combine Mary's $5 million exemption allowance and Jim's $1 million DSUEA. Mary's estate can only exclude $6 million of Mary's taxable estate from federal taxes, even though Mary's estate may include the $5 million of assets she inherited from John, her first husband.
- If Mary does not file Form 706 in a timely manner and claim Jim's $1 million DSUEA, Mary's estate cannot use either John or Jim's DSUEA. Mary's estate could only claim Mary's $5 million personal estate exemption allowance.

Q. *Can domestic partners claim and use the deceased spouse portability exclusion amount?*

A. No. The existing Defense of Marriage Act limits federal benefits to a traditional husband and wife.

Q. *Is the amount of the DSUEA adjusted for inflation?*

A. No. The DSUEA is not indexed for inflation.

WHAT ARE THE FEDERAL ESTATE TAX RATES?

Q. *How do you determine your federal estate tax rates?*

A. The estate tax is a progressive tax levied on the value of the taxable estate exceeding the amount excluded from federal estate taxes, as follows:

Taxable Estate	Estate Tax
• Up to $10,000	18% of excess over excluded amount
• $10,000 to $20,000	$1,800 plus 20% over $10,000
• $20,000 to $40,000	$3,800 plus 22% over $20,000
• $40,000 to $60,000	$8,200 plus 24% over $40,000
• $60,000 to $80,000	$13,00 plus 26% over $60,000
• $80,000 to $100,000	$18,200 plus 28% over $80,000
• $100,000 to $150,000	$23,800 plus 30% over $100,000
• $150,000 to $250,000	$38,800 plus 32% over $150,000
• $250,000 to $500,000	$70,800 plus 34% over $250,000
• $500,001 and over	$155,800 plus 35% over $500,000

If the estate tax reverts back to the 2001 tax laws, the tax table would include additional progressive tax rates, as follows:

• $500,000 to $750,000	$155,800 plus 37% over $500,000
• $750,000 to $1,000,000	$248,300 plus 39% over $750,000
• $1,000,000 to $1,250,000	$345,800 plus 41% over $1,000,000
• $1,250,000 to $1,500,000	$448,300 plus 43% over $1,250,000
• $1,500,000 to $2,000,000	$780,800 plus 49% over $1,500,000
• $2,500,000 to $3,000,000	$1,025,800 plus 53% over $2,500,000
• $3,000,000 and over	$1,290,000 plus 55% over $3,000,000

HOW DO YOU CALCULATE THE AMOUNT OF ESTATE TAXES YOU MIGHT OWE?

Q. *How do you calculate the amount of federal estate tax due?*

A. Federal estate taxes are paid on assets that do not go to a surviving spouse. The estate tax due is determined by applying the applicable tax rate the year of death to the value of the estate in excess of the personal estate tax exemption allowance applicable the year of death. If portability is available, the tax is due on assets that exceed the combined value of the first spouse to die DSUEA and the last spouse to die personal exemption allowance.

In the example below, the taxable value of the estate of the last spouse to die was $7,225,000.

The estate can exclude $7 million of assets from the federal estate tax by combining the last spouse to die $5 million exemption allowance with the first spouse to die $2 million DSUEA.

The net taxable value of the estate is $225,000. If the value of the taxable estate is between $150,000 and $250,000, the federal tax rate is $38,800 plus 32% of any amount over $150,000. The total federal tax due is $62,800.

Step 1. Calculate the taxable value of your estate

Type of Property	Fair Market Value of Asset		Debts		Net Taxable Value
House	$1,500,000	-		=	$1,500,000
Vacation Home		-		=	
Life Insurance Proceeds	$3,000,000	-		=	$3,000,000
Roth Retirement Accounts	$200,000	-		=	$200,000
401(k) Retirement Account	$470,000	-		=	$470,000
Vehicle	$30,000	-	$15,000	=	$15,000
Jewelry		-		=	
Art	$50,000	-		=	$50,000
Collectibles & Coins		-		=	
Personal Property		-		=	
Brokerage Accounts		-		=	
Checking Accounts		-		=	
Mutual Funds		-		=	
Certificate of Deposits		-		=	
Bonds		-		=	
Business Interests		-		=	

Type of Property	Fair Market Value of Asset		Debts		Net Taxable Value
Royalties		-		=	
Rental Property		-		=	
Land		-		=	
Funeral Expenses		-	$10,000	=	-$10,000
Unallowed Gifts		-		=	
Total Taxable Estate Value	**$7,250,000**	**-**	**-$25,000**	**=**	**$7,225,000**

Step 2. Deduct the Personal Estate Tax Exemption Allowance OR the combined Personal Allowance with the Deceased Spouse Unclaimed Exclusion Amount

Total Taxable Estate Value	7,250,000	-	$25,000	=	$7,225,000
2011 Personal Tax Exemption Allowance Deceased Spouse Unclaimed Exclusion Amount		-		=	-$5.000,000 -$2,000,000
Total Value Excluded From Estate Tax **Value of Estate Subject to Estate Tax**		**-**		**=**	**$7,000,000** **$225,000**

Step 3. Determine the appropriate tax rate and calculate the estate tax due

	Fair Market Value	-	Debts	=	Net Taxable Value	Federal Estate Tax Rate
Value of Estate subject to Estate Tax					$225,000	
Federal Estate Tax Due					-$62,800	$38,800 plus 32% over $150,000

	Fair Market Value	-	Debts	=	Net Taxable Value	Federal Estate Tax Rate
State Estate or Inheritance Tax Due					If you instruct your estate to pay these on behalf of the beneficiaries.	Only applicable if the state has an inheritance tax.
Net Available for Distribution to Beneficiaries					**$7,162,200**	

Q. *The value of your estate does not exceed the allowable estate tax personal exemption exclusion, so why should you worry about avoiding the estate tax?*

A. Depending on your age and the gross value of your present holdings, you may find inflation, life insurance proceeds, inheritances and the future value of your assets makes this type of tax planning important for you. Our current estate tax laws are temporary laws. You cannot know what the estate tax exclusion will be in the year you die. You cannot know if you will win the lottery. Tax planning is an essential part of your estate plan.

WHO WILL PAY THE ESTATE TAX?

Q. *If estate taxes are due, how will your estate pay them?*

A. You should leave instructions in your will or trust authorizing the estate representative to pay the estate taxes for your heirs; you can even specify which assets should be used to pay the tax. If you do not leave such instructions they will be paid by the estate representative from assets held in the estate.

If you do not specify which assets to liquidate to pay the estate tax, your estate representative will decide how best to pay the taxes due. When thinking about who gets what, consider the impact of federal estate taxes and state inheritance taxes and how this changes the value of bequests.

A Family Story: Inequitable inheritance due to estate taxes.

Vinnie had two children, Sophia and Brad. Vinnie's estate consisted of two assets with equal value. The balance of Vinnie's IRA retirement account was $3.5 million. Vinnie's personal residence had a fair market value of $3.5 million. Vinnie wanted to share his $7 million estate equally with Sophia and Brad.

Vinnie named Brad as the beneficiary on the IRA beneficiary form. Instructions in Vinnie's will gave Sophia the house. Vinnie's will also included typical default instructions requesting the estate pay any estate taxes due.

Vinnie died in 2011. His estate can exclude $5 million of taxable assets from the federal estate tax, the amount of Vinnie's personal tax exemption allowance. The remaining $2 million will be subject to the federal estate tax. His estate owed $650,800 in estate taxes; $155,800 on the first $500,000 plus 35% on the taxable estate over $500,000.

The inherited IRA was not subject to probate and was not part of Vinnie's probate estate. Brad automatically and immediately inherited the balance of the IRA account, a total of $3.5 million.

The house Sophia inherited was a probate asset. The executor had to hire a lawyer and open a probate case. Sophia could not receive her inheritance until the court was satisfied the estate had paid the estate taxes due. Sophia, a college student, had no assets. The executor had to sell the house in order to pay the estate tax. The estate eventually paid $650,800 for estate taxes and $35,000 foe legal fees. Two years later, Sophia inherited $2,814,200.

When determining who will inherit what, be sure to consider the impact of estate taxes and inheritance taxes on the value of the inheritance.

Fact: Small business estate tax deferral.

If you own a small business it becomes part of your estate at death. Your executor may elect to pay estate tax attributable to the business over fourteen years plus interest on the deferred tax liability.

ARE NON U.S. CITIZENS SUBJECT TO THE FEDERAL ESTATE TAX?

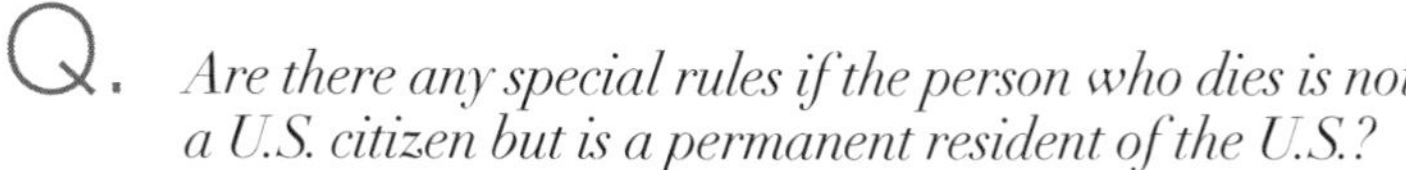

A. Non-citizens residing permanently in the U.S. are subject to federal estate tax assessed on their total worldwide assets. The non-citizen decedent, if a permanent resident, is eligible for the personal federal estate tax exemption allowance.

If you are married, any property you leave to your U.S. citizen spouse is normally exempt from federal estate tax, referred to as the "marital deduction." If the spouse is not a citizen of the United States, the marital exemption is lost, even if the non-citizen spouse was married to a U.S. citizen or is a legal resident of the U.S.

You can, however, leave your non-citizen spouse some property tax free. A non-citizen spouse can claim their personal tax exemption allowance. If the personal tax exemption allowance is $5 million the year you die, the non-citizen spouse can inherit that amount tax free.

If you or your spouse is not a citizen you should seek expert advice in arranging your estate.

WHAT DO YOU NEED TO KNOW ABOUT STATE INHERITANCE TAXES?

Q. *Do states also have an estate tax?*

A. Prior to the 2001 legislation, states received a portion of the federal estate taxes paid. This provision was phased out by 2005 and, as a result, many states have or are considering imposing estate taxes on the estate of the deceased.

In addition, some states impose a state inheritance tax on beneficiaries who inherit property. If any of your beneficiaries live in one of these states, they must report the amount of their inheritance as income when they file their state tax return. Don't plan on dying in a state with an estate or inheritance tax. It will increase your tax bill.

You have the right to provide in your will or your trust that any inheritance taxes will be paid from the estate before the estate is distributed to your beneficiaries.

States may have special rules when spouses and children inherit property; the inheritance tax rate is often lower than the tax rate applied to other beneficiaries. Many states do not collect inheritance taxes from spouses or children.

- If you own real estate in another state, your estate may need to file and pay an estate or inheritance tax in that state.
- Each state sets its own exemption allowance. In New Jersey, the allowance for the years 2011 and 2012 is $675,000.
- Some state inheritance tax laws are tied to the federal estate tax laws. Existing state laws may change again in 2013.
- In some states the executor may be required to obtain an inheritance tax waiver from the state tax

authorities before the assets in the deceased's probate accounts may be released.

States are continuing to change their estate and inheritance tax rules. We recommend you talk with a professional advisor to understand the status of estate and inheritance taxes in your state if you believe the value of your estate will be subject to a state estate or inheritance tax.

Fact: States with estate taxes/inheritance taxes.

Estate Taxes:

The following states have some type of an estate tax: Connecticut, Delaware, Hawaii, Illinois, Maine, Maryland, Massachusetts, Minnesota, New Jersey, New York, North Carolina, Ohio, Oklahoma, Oregon, Rhode Island, Tennessee, Vermont, Washington, Wisconsin, and the District of Columbia.

Inheritance Taxes:

The following states have some type of inheritance tax: Indiana, Iowa, Kansas, Kentucky, Louisiana, Maryland, Nebraska, New Jersey, Pennsylvania, and Tennessee.
ibutton: State Inheritance Taxes diesmart.com/ibutton

Q. *You just inherited money from someone that resides outside the U.S. Do you owe any U.S. taxes on this inheritance?*

A. No tax will be imposed on the inheritance when you receive it because the U.S. federal government does not have an inheritance tax. When you die, money remaining from your inheritance will be included as part of your taxable estate.

If you receive an inheritance or a gift of more than $100,000 from a foreign source it must be reported on Form 3520, Annual Return to Report Transactions With Foreign Trusts and Receipt of Certain Foreign Gifts. This form is an information return; there are no taxes due.

WHEN DO YOU NEED TO FILE THE IRS FORM 706 FEDERAL ESTATE TAX RETURN?

Q. *Under what circumstances must an estate tax return be filed?*

A. Form 706 must be filed if a surviving spouse wants to claim and preserve the deceased spouse unused exclusion amount. Form 706 must also be filed whenever the gross value of the estate exceeds the tax personal exemption allowed the year the decedent dies.

- The gross value is the fair market value of your estate, without any deductions for debts owed and whether or not any estate taxes are payable.
- The taxable value of the estate is the gross value of the estate minus any debts. If the taxable value of your estate exceeds the estate tax personal exemption allowance, estate taxes must be paid when Form 706 is filed.

The Form 706 estate tax return and any tax due must be filed nine months after the date of death. An extension of the Form 706 filing for up to a year past the nine month due date may be granted by the IRS but the estimated estate tax due must be paid on the nine month anniversary of death.

The Internal Revenue Service collects the federal estate tax on all U.S. citizens and residents. The tax is levied on the deceased's estate as a whole and is filed on a single Form 706 federal estate tax return and any taxes due are paid out of the estate's funds.

The IRS carefully reviews each Form 706 filed and will generally give a clearance notification approximately a year after the Form 706 is filed. In many instances the IRS will also audit the last three years' regular Form 1040 submissions of the deceased, inasmuch as this may be the last opportunity to assess additional taxes by the IRS. Once the IRS gives its clearance of a Form 706, it is often necessary for the decedent's representative to send a copy to the state where state death or inheritance returns are filed.

If a probate case is filed, the court will usually not authorize the final distribution of property to the beneficiaries until the estate taxes are paid.

A Family Story: Gross value of estate requires filing Form 706.

Judy died in 2011. The gross value of Judy's estate was $5,250,000. The net taxable estate was $4,425,000. No estate tax was due, as Judy's estate could exclude $5 million of taxable assets from the federal estate tax. Judy's estate must still file a Form 706 tax return as the gross value of the estate exceeded Judy's $5 million personal estate tax exemption allowance

WHAT IS THE MARRIED COUPLE ESTATE TAX TRAP?

Q. *If you are married, are estate taxes due when the first spouse dies?*

A. The first spouse to die may give all of their assets to the surviving spouse without paying any estate tax, no matter what the taxable value of the estate is. This is referred to as the unlimited marital deduction; the first spouse to die has not claimed any of their $5 million estate tax exemption allowance.

The unlimited marital deduction is not available if the surviving spouse is not a U.S. citizen.

An estate tax calculation will be done when the surviving spouse dies, and will be based upon the fair market value of all the assets owned by the surviving spouse, including those inherited from the first spouse.

Q. *What happens to the estate tax personal exemption allowance of the first spouse to die?*

A. The surviving spouse can file Form 706 and preserve the right to use the $5 million DSUEA of the first spouse to die. When the surviving spouse dies, the estate can combine the $5 million DSUEA with the $5 million estate tax exemption allowance of the last spouse to die, potentially excluding $10 million of assets from estate taxes.

If Form 706 is not filed, the surviving spouse loses the right to claim the unused $5 million estate tax exemption allowance of the first spouse to die.

We refer to the failure to file the DSUEA as the married couple estate tax trap.

WHY SHOULD MARRIED COUPLES CONSIDER A MARITAL A/B TRUST?

Q. *Why would married couples consider an A/B trust?*

A. Until the deceased spouse unused exclusion amount became part of the 2010 Tax Relief Act, the only way to preserve the estate tax allowance of the first spouse to die and the last spouse to die was to set up an A/B trust.

You might question whether or not you still need an A/B trust. An A/B trust may be useful for several reasons:

- The deceased spouse unused exclusion amount is a temporary provision and only covers the estates of someone who dies between January 1, 2011 and December 31, 2012.
- Any increase in value of the first spouse to die assets placed in Trust "B" are not subject to tax when the surviving spouse dies.
- State estate taxes did not go away and may not provide a $5 million exclusion amount.

Q. *What is an A/B trust?*

A. Married couples can leave instructions in their will or in their living trust to establish new A/B trusts when the first spouse dies.

In an A/B Trust the marital assets are split and transferred to two separate trusts, known as Trust "A" and Trust "B," created when the first spouse dies.

Q. *What happens with Trust "A"?*

A. Trust "A," which was set up by the surviving spouse, is a revocable trust. The surviving spouse can be trustee and usually has total control over the assets in the trust.

The surviving spouse can generally do with the assets transferred to Trust "A" whatever he or she pleases.

The surviving spouse decides who inherits the assets in Trust "A" when he or she dies, and may change the names of the beneficiaries until he or she dies or becomes incapacitated.

Q. *What happens with Trust "B"?*

A. Trust "B" is set up according to the instructions previously specified in the living trust of the deceased spouse. The new Trust "B" becomes an irrevocable trust upon the death of the first spouse.

The assets in Trust "B" are managed according to the instructions specified in the decedent's living trust agreement. The trustee of Trust "B" is the person the deceased specified in their living trust and commonly is the surviving spouse.

Usually, the income from Trust "B" is used to support the surviving spouse, and the principal is maintained for the benefit of the ultimate beneficiaries of the trust after the surviving spouse dies. Since the Trust "B" is irrevocable, the surviving spouse cannot generally change any terms or instructions defined by the first spouse to die.

Q. *How does an A/B trust save on estate taxes?*

A. The will or the living trust of the first spouse to die instructs the estate representative to transfer to trust "B" property up to the maximum federal estate tax exemption allowable in the year of death.

When the surviving spouse dies, the property in trust "B" is not part of his or her estate, regardless of its value. The deceased spouse's estate only owes estate taxes on trust "A" assets.

If the assets of the first spouse are given directly to the

surviving spouse, any growth in the assets is subject to estate taxes when the surviving spouse dies. There is no adjustment for inflation on the deceased spouse unused exclusion amount. Setting up an A/B trust allows the assets in trust "B" to grow and be distributed tax-free when the second spouse dies no matter what the value.

Q. *What happens if the value of the assets of the first spouse to die exceeds the estate tax personal exemption allowance?*

A. If the value of the property of the first spouse to die exceeds the federal estate tax personal exemption allowance, the first spouse to die has several choices.

Choice 1. If you want to control the distribution of the excess assets when the surviving spouse dies, your trust instructions can provide that the amount of your estate in excess of the estate tax personal exemption allowance be placed in a new trust, commonly referred to as a "C" trust.

The trustee of the "C" trust must manage these assets according to your directions, which can be the same as directions you leave for the "B" trust. For instance, your instructions can direct any income be paid to a surviving spouse and upon his or her death, the "C" trust assets be given to your grandchildren.

Your estate representative must immediately pay estate taxes on the funds set aside in the "C" trust. Similar to the "B" trust, the assets in the "C" trust can continue to grow but no additional estate taxes will be assessed at the time the "C" trust is distributed.

Example: Spouse 1 dies.

The combined value of their marital property is $12 million. The first spouse to die's share of the estate is valued at $6 million. The estate tax exemption allowance is $5 million.

Trust "A" (revocable)	Trust "B" (irrevocable)	Trust "C" (irrevocable)
$6 million of marital assets given to Trust "A".	$5 million of marital assets given to Trust "B".	$1 million of assets given to Trust "C".
The surviving spouse owes no estate taxes, claims the marital tax exemption.	No estate tax is due. The estate claims the first spouse to die $5 million personal estate tax exemption allowance.	Estate taxes due on $1 million when first spouse dies.
	Per the specifications in the living trust of the first spouse to die, income received from trust "B" assets is paid to the surviving spouse as long as the surviving spouse lives.	Per the instructions specified in the living trust of the first spouse to die, income from Trust "C" is paid to surviving spouse during surviving spouse's lifetime.
The surviving spouse sets up Trust "A" and specifies who will inherit Trust "A" assets when he or she dies.	The instructions in the living trust of the first spouse to die specify who will inherit Trust "B" assets when the surviving spouse dies.	The instructions in the living trust of the first spouse to die specify who will inherit Trust "C" assets when the surviving spouse dies.
When the second spouse dies, the estate claims his or her personal estate tax exemption allowance and pays any necessary estate taxes due on assets in Trust "A".	When second spouse dies, Trust "B" assets are distributed according to the instructions specified in the living trust of the first spouse to die. The value of the assets in Trust "B" pass estate tax free to the beneficiaries first spouse to die specified in his or her living trust.	When second spouse dies, assets in trust "C" pass tax free to the beneficiaries first spouse to die specified in his or her living trust.

Choice 2. Your trust instructions can provide the excess assets be given to the "A" trust. The excess assets will now be under the control of the surviving spouse. The distribution of the assets will be done according to the terms of the "A" trust when the surviving spouse dies.

No estate taxes are due on the excess assets. When the surviving spouse dies, all of the assets in the "A" trust will be subject to any applicable estate taxes.

Example: Spouse 1 dies.

The combined value of your marital estate is $12 million. The first spouse to die's share of the estate is valued at $6 million. The estate tax exemption allowance the year of death is $5 million.

Trust "A" (revocable)	Trust "B" (revocable)
$7 million of marital assets transferred to Trust "A". The $7 million represents surviving spouse share ($6 million) of the marital assets plus the value of the first spouse to die marital assets that exceed the estate tax exemption allowance of the first spouse to die ($1 million).	$5 million of marital assets are transferred to trust "B". The $5 million is the amount of the federal tax exemption allowance available the year the first spouse died
The surviving spouse owes no estate taxes, claims the marital tax exemption.	No estate tax is due because the first spouse to die claims his or her $5 million estate tax federal exemption allowance.
The surviving spouse sets up Trust "A" and specifies who will inherit Trust "A" assets when he or she dies.	Per the instructions specified in the living trust of the first spouse to die, income from Trust "B" is paid to surviving spouse during spouse's lifetime.
When second spouse dies, all Trust "A" assets are distributed according to the wishes of second spouse to die.	When second spouse dies, Trust B assets are distributed according to instructions specified in the living trust of the first spouse to die.
When the second spouse dies, the estate claims his or her personal estate tax allowance and pays any necessary estate taxes due on assets in Trust "A".	When second spouse dies, trust "B" is not considered part of the estate of the second spouse to die and is not subject to any additional estate tax. If Trust "B" assets have a value of $6 million when the second spouse dies, none of the $6 million is subject to federal estate tax.

HOW CAN A LIFE INSURANCE TRUST MINIMIZE YOUR ESTATE TAX?

Q. *Are your life insurance proceeds subject to estate tax?*

A. If you are the owner of the policy, or can designate beneficiaries, life insurance proceeds are considered part of your taxable estate. Owning a sizable life insurance policy can trigger or greatly increase federal estate taxes. Unless they own the policy, beneficiaries who receive life insurance proceeds do not have to pay income tax on these proceeds because those same benefits are included as part of your taxable estate.

Q. *Is there a way to eliminate estate taxes on life insurance benefits?*

A. A life insurance or financial services advisor can help design an Irrevocable Life Insurance Trust. Premiums are paid by the trust from gifts made to the trust during the life of the insured. Because the insured does not own the trust or have any control over the trust, the policy is not part of the insured's estate.

The trust can be designed to accumulate the income earned on the death benefit after its payment to a surviving spouse until death. Thereafter, the trust principal can be distributed to heirs without any tax. The distributions to heirs can be restricted until they attain 46 years of age.

The trust must be irrevocable. If you transfer a life insurance policy into a life insurance trust, but die within three years of the transfer, the policy ownership reverts to your estate and the estate pays tax on the proceeds. The value of your life insurance will be included as part of your taxable estate any time you keep the right to change the name of the beneficiary on the trust's policy.

HOW CAN GIFT LAWS HELP MINIMIZE YOUR ESTATE TAXES?

Q. *How can gifting minimize estate taxes?*

A. Taking advantage of "gifting" can be a way for you to reduce the size of your estate tax bill and can benefit both you and your children and grandchildren. A regular gift giving program can result in substantial cumulative transfers of assets over the years.

If you have a substantial estate, "gifting" can reduce the taxable value of your estate and reduce the amount of estate taxes owed when you die. Under existing estate tax rates, every dollar you can move out of your estate could save your heirs up to thirty-five cents if you died in 2010 or 2011.

Gift tax laws allow you to give away a certain amount of money each year tax-free. The gift tax laws are comprised of three sets of tax giving rules: the annual gift tax exclusion, direct gifts for education and medical expenses, and the $5 million lifetime tax-free gift allowance.

ANNUAL GIFT EXCLUSION

Q. *What is the annual gift tax exclusion?*

A. Each of us is allowed to give a certain amount of cash or property to an unlimited number of recipients tax-free each year. In 2011 and 2012, the annual gift allowance is $13,000 for each person. The amount of the gift tax exclusion is set by the IRS and is adjusted each year.

These gifts are not income to the recipient, nor do you get a tax deduction for them. You can give amounts up to the amount of the gift allowance to as many people as you want, without triggering the gift tax.

A Family Story: Tax-free gifts.

Ross and Jessica are married. They have children, Eric and Clark.

In December, 2010, Ross gave $13,000 to Eric and $13,000 to Clark as a Christmas present. Jessica also gave $13,000 to Eric and $13,000 to Clark as a Christmas present.

The gift tax exclusion rule allows everyone to give away the amount of the annual gift exclusion each year to multiple recipients. None of these gifts triggered a tax event for the recipients, so Eric and Clark do not have to report the gifts as income or pay income taxes on the gifts. Ross and Jessica get no tax deduction, but have reduced the size of their taxable estate by $52,000.

DIRECT GIFTS FOR EDUCATION AND MEDICAL EXPENSES

Q. *Are direct gifts of tuition and medical fees part of the annual gift tax calculations?*

A. No. In addition to gifts, you can pay certain educational and health related expenses on behalf of others with no tax consequences. The gift tax laws allow you to make a direct payment to an educational institution for tuition on behalf of your children or grandchildren. To be considered tax-free gifts payment must be made directly to the educational institution and must be for tuition only.

You can also pay certain medical expenses, including medical insurance, diagnosis, and treatment of diseases, but these payments also must be made directly to the care provider or insurer.

A Family Story: Tax-free gifts.

Jeff and Annie are married. They have two grandchildren attending college, Joe and Emma.

In January, 2011, Jeff decided to pay their tuition. Jeff sent a check for $25,000 payable to Stanford University for Emma's tuition and a check for $25,000 payable to UCLA for Joe's tuition.

In March, 2011, Emma broke her leg playing soccer and incurred $5,000 of medical bills. Annie made a check payable to the hospital where Emma was treated in the amount of $5,000.

In December, 2011, Jeff gave Emma $13,000 and Joe $13,000 as a Christmas gift. Annie also gave Emma $13,000 and Joe $13,000 as a Christmas gift.

In the year 2011, Jeff and Annie made gifts of $105,000: $50,000 for tuition, $5,000 for medical expenses and $52,000 as Christmas gifts.

None of these gifts triggered a tax event for the recipients. Joe and Emma did not have to report any income on their tax returns. Jeff and Annie reduced the size of their taxable estate by $105,000, potentially saving thousands of dollars in estate taxes.

None of these gifts are considered part of Jeff's or Annie's $5 million lifetime gift tax allowance.

THE $5 MILLION LIFETIME GIFT ALLOWANCE

Q. *What is the $5 million lifetime gift tax allowance?*

A. The gift tax laws also include a lifetime $5 million gift tax allowance, giving each of us the right to give away $5 million of gifts while we are living without having to pay any gift tax.

- The $5 million gift tax allowance is in addition to the free gifts you can make using the annual gift tax exclusions rules and the direct payment of tuition and medical expenses.

- The $5 million of gifts can be made in multiple years and to multiple individuals.

- If you are married, a husband and a wife each have a $5 million allowance, giving a married couple a $10 million lifetime gift allowance.

Why would you want to give away $5 million before you die? The reason is simple – to get it out of your estate and into the hands of your heirs. If you keep the $5 million, it will be subject to estate tax rules. If you give it to your children, neither the principal nor the growth will ever be subject to your estate taxes.

A Family Story: $5,000,000 tax-free allowance.

Sheldon started an internet company when he was very young, which was subsequently acquired by a Fortune 1000 company.

Sheldon decided to give his two adult children, Samuel and Samantha, the benefit of his entrepreneurial success while they were young, rather than after he died.

Sheldon gave Samantha and Samuel each $500,000 from the proceeds of the sale of the company, taking advantage of his $5 million lifetime gift tax allowance. Samuel and Samantha do not owe taxes on the $500,000. Sheldon gets no tax deduction, but has reduced his taxable estate by $1 million.

The personal estate tax exemption allowed when someone dies is a combination of the lifetime gift tax allowance and the estate tax *exemption allowance. Since Sheldon used $1 million of his lifetime gift tax allowance while he was living, his estate must deduct $1 million from his $5 million personal tax exemption allowance. When Sheldon dies, Sheldon's estate can only claim a $4 million personal estate tax exemption.*

Q. *Why can't you give away all your assets and avoid paying any estate tax?*

A. The IRS provides a life time gift tax allowance of $5 million. If the cumulative total of your gifts exceeds $5 million you must pay a gift tax.

- Adding a joint tenant to real estate is considered a taxable gift if the new joint tenant has the right under state law to sell his interest and receive half of the property.

- Adding a joint tenant to a bank or brokerage account or to a U.S. Savings bond is not considered to be a gift until the new joint tenant withdraws funds.

- If you purchase a security in the names of the joint owners, rather than holding it in street name by the brokerage firm, the amount of the transaction would be considered a taxable gift.

The tax basis for gifts is different than the tax basis for inherited property. The recipient of the gift must carry forward the same tax basis as the person giving the property for purpose of calculating future capital gains or losses when the property is sold. The recipient of inherited property receives a "stepped up" basis equal to the fair market value of the property on the date of death of the owner, which is used to calculate a capital gain or a capital loss when the property is sold.

The gift tax rate in 2011 and 2012 is 35% of any gifts given in excess of $5 million.

You will pay taxes if you make excessive gifts before you die, or you will owe estate taxes if the property is part of your taxable estate when you die.

Q. *Are gifts between husband and wife reportable?*

A. Gifts of any amount between husband and wife are not reportable providing they are both U.S. citizens.

You must file a Form 709 Gift Tax return if you gave a non-citizen spouse over $125,000 in a single year. The $125,00 is referred to as the Annual Tax Exclusion Amount. The Annual Tax Exclusion Amount is set by Congress and changes each year. In 2010, the exclusion amount is $125,000.

Q. *Are there any tax reporting requirements for gifts?*

A. If you make a gift of more than $13,000 directly to a person, you need to file IRS Form 709, U.S. Gift (and Generation Skipping Transfer) Tax Return, which is due April 15 of the following year. You owe no gift tax unless the cumulative total of your excess gifts reported on Form 709 exceeds your lifetime $5 million gift tax allowance.

You can continue making gifts to individuals in excess of the $5,000,000. Once your lifetime gift tax allowance is used up, you pay a gift tax when you file your Form 709.

Q. *How is your estate tax exposure affected by the value of gifts that you give?*

A. Annual Gift Rules

Your annual gifts in 2011 did not exceed $13,000 to any one person.	Your annual gifts in 2011 to one person exceeded $13,000.
You do not need to file Form 709 when you complete your tax return. Your gifts do not exceed the $13,000 a year limit and have no impact on the calculation of your estate taxes.	You need to document the gift on Form 709 and file it with your 1040 tax return. Save a copy of the 709 tax return with your estate filing system. When someone is calculating your estate tax, they will need to deduct the amount of the gifts made exceeding $13,000 per person per year from the federal personal tax exemption allowance.

In 2013, the lifetime gift allowance reverts to $1 million and the gift tax rate reverts to 55% unless Congress extends our temporary estate tax laws or changes existing law.

Bottom Line:

If you are married, don't fall into the married couple estate tax trap.

Grandparents, take advantage of the gift tax rules and help pay college tuition for your grandchildren.

Action Checklist: Take steps to minimize any estate taxes due.

- ❑ If you are married with significant assets and want to leave assets for the benefit of children from a first marriage, consider setting up an A/B trust.
- ❑ If you are married and your spouse dies, DO NOT FORGET to file a deceased spouse unused exclusion amount form 706 with the Internal Revenue Service.
- ❑ Use the gift tax allowance to help pay for education for your grandchildren.
- ❑ If you have key man insurance or other significant life insurance policies, talk to a lawyer about placing the ownership of the policies in an irrevocable trust.
- ❑ Pay attention to Congress. They will be making changes to the current temporary federal estate tax laws.
- ❑ Pay attention to state inheritance taxes. Don't die in New Jersey. The New Jersey estate tax may cost more than the federal estate tax.

Mistake #7
You heard if you had a will you could skip probate

Words to Know:

- Contingent Beneficiary
- Contract Law
- Intestate Succession
- Joint Tenants In Common
- Joint Tenants In Entirety
- Joint Tenants with Rights of Survivorship
- Living Trusts
- Per Capita
- Per Stirpes
- Primary Beneficiary
- Probate Assets
- Property Title

A Family Story: A will did not avoid probate.

Judy and George Adams owned their personal residence as joint tenants with the right of survivorship. Judy died first. Upon Judy's death, as a matter of law, George, as the surviving joint tenant, became the automatic owner of the real estate. Since the real estate was not a probate asset, the county recorder did not require any documents from the probate court when George requested the name on the deed be changed from Judy and George Adams to George Adams.

George died several years later. As the last surviving joint tenant, the property was considered to be owned by George as an individual. The real estate is a probate asset, managed by the instructions in George's will.

George's will named his son, Jason, to inherit the property. When Jason requested the county recorder to change the name on the deed from George Adams to Jason Adams, Jason needed to include an order signed by the judge of the probate court giving Jason the legal right to change the name on the deed. Jason could not obtain such an order without first opening a probate case.

WHAT YOU WILL LEARN IN THIS CHAPTER

Title is the manner in which both real and personal property is owned. Title may be proven by certificate, deed, bill of sale, contract, signature cards or other documents. The title documents may also designate a beneficiary.

The title may state an individual owns the property or

multiple people own the property, i.e., joint tenants with rights of survivorship, or a trust owns the property.

It turns out title is more than a piece of paper conveying ownership of a house, a car or a safe deposit box. Property title determines whether contract law governs the inheritance of the property or whether the wishes written in your will or trust govern the inheritance of the property.

This chapter explains how title determines whether your estate is subject to probate, what probate is, and how you can title property to avoid probate.

WHAT ARE ASSET BUCKETS AND WHY DO THEY MATTER?

Q. *What do you mean by an asset bucket?*

A. When you die, someone will make an inventory of your estate. Think of your titled assets as going into three buckets: the probate bucket, the trust bucket and the automatic inheritance bucket. Which bucket the asset belongs in is determined by the way the property is titled.

Probate Assets

- Property owned by an individual.
- Property owned as joint tenants with rights of survivorship, no living joint tenant.
- Property where "Estate" is the named beneficiary or becomes the default beneficiary because the designated beneficiary died before the owner.
- The decedent's share of property owned as tenants in common.

Trust Assets

- Property owned by a trustee.

Automatic inheritance assets:

- Joint tenants with right of survivorship, a living joint tenant.
- Community property with right of survivorship, a living joint tenant.
- Property owned by an individual, or more than one person with a designated living beneficiary: life insurance policies, retirement accounts, pay on death bank accounts, transfer on death brokerage accounts and transfer on death real estate deeds and vehicle registration forms.

Q. *Why do the buckets matter?*

A. Once you know in what bucket the asset belongs you will know who has the authority to empty the bucket.

- Probate assets will be managed by the executor named in your will or by a personal representative appointed by the court if you do not have a will.
    - Instructions in your will generally determine the beneficiary of your probate assets. If you do not have a will, state intestate succession rules determine the beneficiary.
    - The executor or personal representative must determine what type of probate procedures are required to get authority (Letters or Affidavits) to manage the property.
- Trust assets will be managed by the successor trustee named in your trust.
    - Instructions in your trust determine who are the beneficiaries of assets owned by your trust.
    - The trust gives the successor trustee the legal authority to manage trust assets.

- Assets with automatic inheritance rights will be managed by the beneficiaries who automatically inherit the property.
    - The law automatically determines the beneficiaries and overrides any instructions contained in a will or trust.
    - A beneficiary has the authority to immediately claim their property with a certified death certificate and an affidavit or other claim form.

THE THREE PROPERTY BUCKETS (property title)

	The probate bucket:	The trust bucket:	The automatic inheritance bucket:
Property title	Property is owned by an individual. Property where "estate" is the designated beneficiary. Property where "estate" is the default beneficiary because the designated beneficiaries are dead. Joint tenants with rights of survivorship, no living joint tenant.	Property is titled in the name of a trustee.	Joint tenants with rights of survivorship, a living joint tenant. Property owned by an individual, or more than one person, with a designated beneficiary: life insurance policies, 401(k) and IRA accounts, annuities, savings bonds, payable upon death bank accounts, transfer on death brokerage accounts and transfer on death deeds and vehicle registration forms.

	The probate bucket:	The trust bucket:	The automatic inheritance bucket:
Beneficiary procedure to empty the buckets	A will determines who inherits the property. If no will, state intestate succession rules determine the owner. The property is a probate asset and subject to probate. The estate representative manages the transfer of property to the beneficiary. The value of the probate property will determine whether the estate representative can manage the assets with an Affidavit or requires Letters issued by the probate court.	A trust determines who inherits the property. The property is not subject to probate. The trustee manages the transfer of property to the beneficiary.	Contract law determines who inherits the property. The property is not subject to probate. A family member can immediately assist the beneficiary to claim the property.

WHAT HAPPENS WITH PROPERTY PLACED IN THE AUTOMATIC INHERITANCE RIGHTS BUCKET?

A Family Story: Ex-wife is listed as the designated beneficiary.

If you watch Desperate Housewives, you are familiar with the story of Karen McCluskey, the neighborhood witch.

Karen found her husband dead in the middle of the night and elected to call the funeral home the next morning. While reviewing her husband's legal documents, Karen discovered a beneficiary form naming his ex-wife as the beneficiary of his retirement plan, an ex-wife he was married to for three months, 30 years ago. In a moment of panic, Karen decided to put her dead husband in the freezer, keeping the pension payments intact.

Although we may not go to such extremes, it is a fact, barring costly litigation, that the person named on your beneficiary form is the person who will inherit this asset, even if you forgot you did it, even if you are no longer married to this person.

Karen understood the implication of not being named as the beneficiary on the beneficiary form. Generally, the person named on the beneficiary form automatically inherits these assets, regardless of whether his or her will or living trust includes specific instructions giving the asset to someone else.

Q. *What types of property have automatic inheritance rights?*

A. The fact is some of our most valuable assets are governed by other laws that override any instructions we may have written in our will or trusts, or state laws of intestate succession if you do not have a will.

In this case, the rule on who inherits the property is managed by contract law, not our will. For example:

- If you own life insurance or annuities, when you die the proceeds will pass by contract to a living named beneficiary or beneficiaries you designated when you purchased the life insurance policy.

- If you own 401(k), IRA or Roth IRA retirement accounts, when you die these assets also automatically pass by contract to the living named beneficiary or beneficiaries designated on the beneficiary forms. This person or people now owns the asset. However, surviving spouses have certain rights to retirement accounts that cannot be given away without their permission.

- If you own real property with another individual as joint tenants with right of survivorship, the law generally grants automatic inheritance rights to the surviving joint tenant.

Each of these is an example of instances in which the manner in which the assets are titled governs how they are distributed upon your death. Upon your death, the assets pass automatically to someone else. These assets do not exist in your estate and are not subject to your will or probate.

DOES PROPERTY TITLED AS JOINT TENANTS WITH RIGHTS OF SURVIVORSHIP HAVE AUTOMATIC INHERITANCE RIGHTS?

A Family Story: Joint tenancy contract law overrides instructions in a will or trust.

Sue and her sister Brooke decided to pool their money and purchase *a vacation home in Lake Tahoe. They each paid $150,000 to buy the property. The property deed listed the property owners as Sue and Brooke, joint tenants with right of survivorship.*

Sue died first. In her will, Sue bequeathed all of her property, including her half of the vacation property, to her only child, Julie.

If you own real property with another individual as joint tenants with rights of survivorship, contract law grants automatic inheritance rights to the surviving joint tenants. No matter what your will says.

Since the deed named Sue and Brooke as joint tenants with rights of survivorship, Sue presumptively gave her share of the vacation home to Brooke when Sue died. Brooke now owns 100% of the vacation property, despite what Sue's will says. Barring costly litigation, Julie does not inherit Sue's half of the property.

Q. *Who inherits property owned as joint tenants with the right of survivorship when the first joint tenant dies?*

A. Joint tenancy is one way in which property can be titled. Joint tenancy generally means that each joint tenant has the right to 100% of the property. When one joint tenant dies, the remaining joint tenant is the sole owner of the entire property.

This notion that the surviving joint tenant enjoys complete ownership of the tenancy is called "the right of survivorship." Most states presume that property held in joint tenancy includes the right of survivorship.

When property is held in joint tenancy and one of the joint tenants dies, the right of complete ownership is vested in the surviving joint tenant. The decedent's former interest in the property is generally not subject to a will, trust or probate, because the interest is lost upon the death of the decedent.

So, if you own property as a joint tenant, do not assume

that by identifying the property in your will or trust, you have arranged to pass on your interest in the property. To the contrary, since the property is held in joint tenancy, there is a presumption that the property automatically transfers to someone else upon your death.

Q. *Who inherits property titled as joint tenants with right of survivorship when the last surviving joint tenant dies?*

A. When the first tenant dies, the property becomes the property of the surviving joint tenant. When the surviving joint tenant dies, the property is considered owned by that individual. The property has no automatic inheritance rights when the surviving joint tenant dies and may be considered a probate asset of the last joint tenant to die.

If the last surviving joint tenant has a will, the beneficiaries named in the will may inherit the property. If the last surviving joint tenant dies intestate, state laws determine who inherits the property.

DOES PROPERTY WITH A DESIGNATED BENEFICIARY HAVE AUTOMATIC INHERITANCE RIGHTS?

A Family Story: Beneficiary basics.

Hanna and Jake, a married couple, have children from a prior marriage.

Hanna and Jake each own an individual retirement account (IRA). Hanna and Jake both want to provide for each other, but also want their children from prior marriages to inherit their retirement accounts upon the death of the second spouse. Jake names Hanna as the primary beneficiary of his IRA and his children from his first marriage as the contingent beneficiaries. Hanna names Jake as the primary beneficiary of her IRA and her children from her first marriage as the contingent beneficiaries.

Both Hanna and Jake's wills specify the surviving spouse will receive income from the retirement account. When the surviving spouse dies, their children from their first marriages will inherit the retirement account.

Hanna and Jake did not take into account beneficiary law. Beneficiary law automatically determines the beneficiary and overrides any instructions in the living trust.

If Hanna dies first, the named primary beneficiary, Jake, automatically becomes the owner of Hanna's retirement account. The contingent beneficiaries named no longer have a claim to the asset. As the new owner, Jake names new beneficiaries for the IRA Jake inherits from Hanna. Jake can name Hanna's children as his beneficiaries, but has the option to name the beneficiary of his choice. If Jake fails to name a new beneficiary for the IRA he inherited from Hanna, it becomes even more complicated. If Jake has remarried, the custodian agreement may give inheritance rights to Jake's new wife.

Q. *What is a designated beneficiary?*

A. You can designate a specific person or persons as the beneficiary who is to receive the specific asset upon your death when you open certain accounts, including bank accounts, brokerage accounts, retirement accounts and insurance policies. Some states allow you to name a beneficiary on a deed or on a vehicle registration form.

Upon your death, your interest in the asset ceases to exist and the beneficiary's interest vests. In such a case, these assets are not subject to probate because you had no ownership interest in the asset which survived your death.

If the assets are jointly owned, the designated living beneficiary automatically inherits the property when the last owner dies.

Just as important, the designated beneficiary is now the rightful owner of the property. Their will or their living trust will determine who inherits the asset when they die.

A Family Story: Pay-On-Death beneficiary form overrides the wishes in a will.

Flossie was in her eighties. She never trusted banks. Her entire net worth of $40,000 was sitting in a box in her closet. James, the oldest son, convinced Flossie that the cash would be safer in a checking account. When Flossie opened her checking account, she signed a Pay On Death (POD) beneficiary form naming Jim as the only beneficiary.

Flossie died two years later. Flossie had two other children, Lawrence and Mary. Her will left instructions to divide her estate equally between Jim, Lawrence and Mary

Jim was the only child listed as a beneficiary on the POD form. Jim inherited all of the money in the bank account, which represented the entire estate. His brother and sister inherited nothing, even though this was not the intention of Flossie. Lawrence and Mary are not talking to Jim.

Q. *What if the beneficiary form cannot be found when you die?*

A. Most contracts include language on what happens if the beneficiary form cannot be found. Some retirement plan custodian agreements presume the retirement account belongs to a surviving spouse. Other contracts may designate your estate as the beneficiary. The asset will be subject to probate. Your will or state intestate succession rules will determine the beneficiary.

For these reasons, when you sign any form designating a beneficiary, ask what would happen if a copy can't be found.

Designating a Minor Child as the Beneficiary

Q. *If you name a minor child as a beneficiary on a beneficiary form, what happens to the automatic inheritance rights?*

A. A minor child cannot own money or property. If you have not named a custodian on the beneficiary form, a guardian of the estate may need to be appointed to manage the asset on behalf of the minor child.

If you have named a minor child as a beneficiary of an asset, someone will need to petition the courts and request a guardian be named to manage any inheritance intended for the minor child.

The asset will be given to your minor child when he or she becomes an adult by state law, usually at either 18 or 21 years of age.

Designating your estate as the beneficiary

Q. *If you list your estate as the beneficiary on a beneficiary form, what happens to the automatic inheritance rights?*

A. If you designate your estate as a beneficiary, there is no "person" to inherit the property. Naming the estate as your beneficiary eliminates any automatic inheritance rights. The property is considered part of your probate estate and will be subject to probate. The instructions in your will determine who inherits the property. If you have no will, state intestacy laws determine who will inherit the asset.

Fact: IRA impact when your estate is the beneficiary.

If you own an individual retirement account (IRA) and your estate is named as the beneficiary or is the contingent beneficiary because your named beneficiaries died before you did, your will determines who inherits your IRA. These beneficiaries lose the ability to stretch the distribution of your retirement account using their life expectancy factor.

WHAT HAPPENS IF A DESIGNATED BENEFICIARY DIES?

Q. *What is a contingent beneficiary?*

A. Most beneficiary forms allow you to specify a primary beneficiary and a contingent beneficiary. If the primary beneficiary dies before you do, the contingent beneficiary will directly inherit the property upon your death.

If the designated primary beneficiary and you die at the same time and you have not listed a contingent beneficiary, your estate may become the default beneficiary. The same rules apply as if you named your estate as the designated beneficiary. The residuary individuals named in your will inherit the property. If you do not have a will, state intestate succession laws will determine who inherits the property.

When you name a designated beneficiary, you should always name an alternate or contingent beneficiary. Sometimes it is not easy to see how to do this on the forms you are signing. Ask your lawyer how you can name an alternate or contingent beneficiary.

Contingent beneficiaries are especially important for 401(k) and other retirement accounts, as the lack of a contingent beneficiary can have a major impact under retirement account distribution laws and can trigger adverse tax consequences for the beneficiaries of your estate.

A Family Story: No contingent beneficiary

Ernie and Ruth, husband and wife, named each other as the beneficiary of their individual 401(k) retirement accounts, but did not name a contingent beneficiary. Ernie and Ruth died together in a plane crash.
Since they were the beneficiaries of each other's account, and they did not name a contingent beneficiary, their company plan identified their estates as the default contingent beneficiaries. The retirement account is now subject to probate.

The probate court becomes involved in distributing the retirement account to the beneficiaries. The value of the inherited 401(k) account will be reduced by the cost of probate, which can be as much as 8% of the value of the 401(k) account in some states. The funds could be tied up in the courts for four months and maybe longer.

Q. *What happens if you list your two children as designated beneficiaries and one of them dies before you do?*

A. The rights of the families of children who die before you do depend on the designation you make regarding their rights.

You could provide that any child who does not survive you loses their right to inherit. If your child had children of their own at the time of their death, these grandchildren would not inherit anything from you because their parent had not survived you.

Or, you could provide that a child who predeceases you and is survived by their own children may have their children inherit some share. In such a case, the amount of inheritance to such children is governed by one of two concepts: per capita or per stirpes division.

- "Per capita" means "by the head." If one of your primary beneficiaries dies before you do, his or her share will be equally distributed to his or her heirs. If you list your children, Ray and Steve, as beneficiaries, each primary beneficiary is entitled to 50 percent of the assets. If Ray has three children the estate will now be divided in four equal shares, because there are "four heads" among whom to distribute the estate.

- "Per stirpes" means "by the group." If one of your primary beneficiaries dies before you do, the size of his share will be limited to that which he would have inherited. If he has three children and he was entitled to 50% of the estate, his children will divide his or her 50%.

As an example, assume you name your children, Ray and Steve, as your beneficiaries. You specify each child will inherit 50% of your estate. Ray has three children, Lucy, Laurie and Luke. Steve has one child, Lily.

When you die, your estate is worth $120,000. If both Ray and Steve were alive, each would inherit $60K. If Ray dies before you or at the same time as you, his share is distributed as follows:

		Per Capita			Per Stirpes		
Ray (deceased)			Steve $30K	Ray (deceased)			Steve $60K
Lucy $30k	Laurie $30k	Luke $30k		Lucy $20k	Laurie $20k	Luke $20k	

Some custodian agreements, or beneficiary form agreements provided by banks and brokerage accounts, may include default language describing whether your beneficiaries will inherit on a per stirpes or a per capita basis. Before writing the names of your beneficiaries on the beneficiary form, ask whether the asset will be distributed on per capita or per stirpes basis if a named beneficiary dies before you do. If you want an exception to the default beneficiaries provided by per capita or per stirpes, talk with an attorney.

Q. *Can you name a trustee of a trust as a beneficiary?*

A. Yes, you can name a trustee of a trust as a beneficiary. If your retirement account (IRA) names a trustee as the beneficiary, the trustee will receive income from the IRA after you die. The instructions in the trust will dictate who receives the asset and who the successor beneficiaries are.

For Jake and Hanna (see story, page 136), an IRA trust would have allowed Jake and Hanna to meet their objectives. If Hanna died first, trust instructions would have provided Jake with income from Hanna's inherited retirement account until he died. When Jake dies, the instructions in the trust would transfer the benefits to Hanna's children.

If you intend to name a trustee as the beneficiary, talk with an attorney.

Q. *Can you disinherit your spouse or children by naming other beneficiaries?*

A. There are generally state and federal rules preventing someone from disinheriting a spouse. Each state has different rules regarding the rights of spouses. You should consult a competent attorney regarding spousal rights.

WHAT HAPPENS WITH PROPERTY PLACED IN THE TRUST BUCKET?

Q. *Who has the authority to manage trust assets?*

A. The co-trustee or successor trustee continues to manage trust assets according to instructions contained in the living trust.

Trust assets are not subject to probate.

WHAT HAPPENS WITH PROPERTY PLACED IN THE PROBATE BUCKET?

Q. *Is probate required if you have a will?*

A. Some people are surprised to discover that having a will does not avoid probate. The fact is probate may not be required even if you die without a will. The need for probate is dependent upon whether your estate includes assets in the probate bucket.

Q. *What is probate?*

A. Probate is a legal process for settling the debts of someone who has died and distributing the remaining property to rightful heirs.

The probate process generally involves use of a set of specific forms, time lines and procedures which vary depending on the state and county where a probate case is filed.

During a probate process, a judge supervises the actions your estate representative makes, such as:

- Gathering your assets so they may be distributed.
- Notifying heirs and creditors of the administration of your estate.

- Accounting for your assets and debts, and payment of creditors and taxes.
- Paying of administrative fee and attorney's fee.
- Distributing your probate property to your heirs.

Q. *What if you die without a will?*

A. There are two types of probate estates, testate and intestate. An intestate estate is the procedure used when you die without a will. Testate is the procedure used when you die with a will.

If you die with a will, the will controls who receives the decedent's assets and the will names an executor who manages the probate process. If you die without a will, state intestate succession laws decide who receives the decedent's assets. State laws also determine who the court appoints as the personal representative to manage the probate process.

Q. *Why is probate required?*

A. The intent of probate is to assure that the heirs and creditors receive their rightful share of a decedent's estate. The states have created the process of "probate" to assure that certain people get notice of the administration of a decedent's estate to allow them to make a claim, and for the court to oversee and hold accountable a person responsible for the collection and distribution of a decedent's assets.

The probate process also appoints a personal representative for the deceased. Official court documents give the appointed representative the legal authority to transact business on behalf of the deceased. During life, the deceased signs deeds or checks. After death, someone must have the authority to act on behalf of the deceased.

The Three Buckets

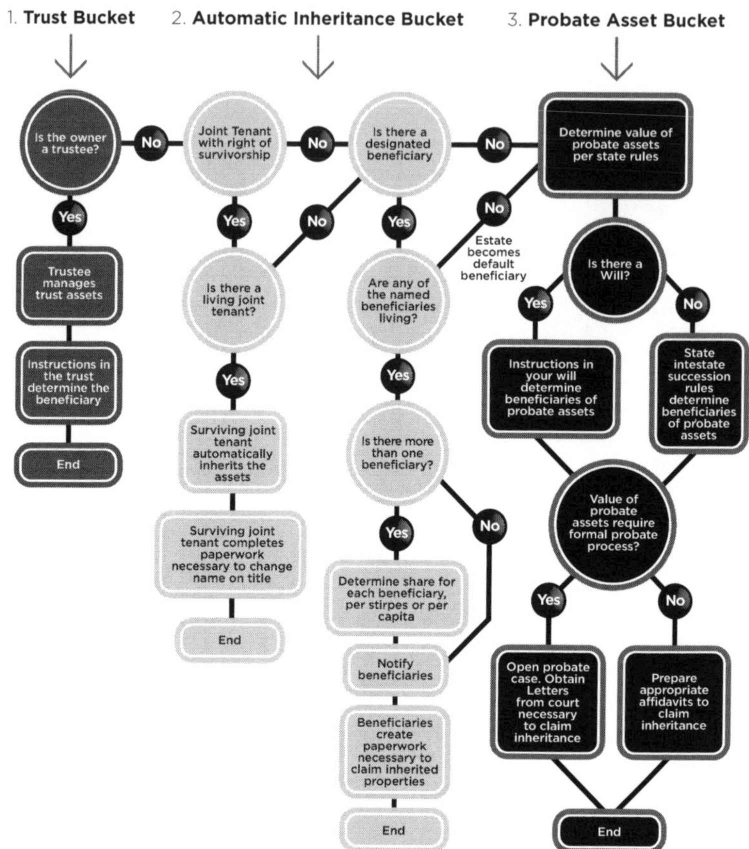

WHY DOESN'T A WILL AVOID PROBATE?

Q. *Does your estate have assets placed in the probate bucket?*

A. Your will directs the disposition of your probate property after you die. If your estate includes probate assets, your will or state intestate succession laws generally direct the distribution of the assets to the new beneficiaries.

Your estate representative will be required to report to the court that the proposed distribution of your assets will specifically follow the terms of your will. The court will then sign documents empowering the estate representative to transfer each asset's title to the beneficiary named in the will.

County recorders and others require documents from the probate court authorizing the transfer of title from the name of the deceased to the new beneficiary.

WHAT DOES PROBATE COST?

Q. *What will it cost your estate if probate is required?*

A. Billions of dollars are spent each year for probate. Probate costs include court costs, estate representative costs, executor fees, attorney fees, bond fees and appraisal fees. In some states, the costs of probate can consume four to eight percent of the value of assets subject to probate.

There is a wide variance in what it can cost your heirs to open and file a probate case. Examples of such fees and costs include the following:

- The statutory fees your attorney and estate representative charge. Some states set "reasonable fees" as the statutory rate. Others set the statutory fees paid to attorneys or executors as a percentage of the gross value of the estate.

- The types of services the attorney performs. Besides statutory fees allowed for completing and filing probate forms with the courts, attorneys have the right to seek payment for "extraordinary services performed" whereby they deliver value to the estate due to unusually difficult or complicated circumstances posed by the probate. For instance, attorneys can charge an extraordinary fee if they are asked to review real estate sales documents. This task is not part of the normal statutory probate fee.

- The type of real estate you own. If you own real estate in another state or another county, it may be necessary to open a second probate case in that state and county and pay additional attorney fees and probate filing fees.

- The cost of a professional testamentary trustee (a trustee of a trust created by a will). If through your will you create a Testamentary Trust, the trustee also has the right to charge the statutory or reasonable fees allowed by the state and/or contemplated by the testamentary trust provisions.

- The fees the courts charge to open a probate case. Some states base court fees on a percentage of the gross value of your probate assets.

- The cost of buying a Surety Bond for your executor, which is paid from your probate assets.

- Whether the surviving spouse is subject to probate. If so, the surviving spouse may be able avoid normal probate procedures and use simplified procedures set up specifically for surviving spouses.

Fact: Estimated probate costs.

Available research shows probate costs can consume between one to eight percent of the value of your probate estate when you die.

Q. *Does your estate representative need to hire an attorney to file a probate case?*

A. Many of us have learned how to do our tax returns. Some of us are willing to learn how to complete the right forms when someone dies.

Some states only allow attorneys to file a probate case. Other states, including California, Maryland and New Hampshire allow your estate representative to fill out and file most required legal forms. **ibutton:** Probate Self Filing diesmart.com/ibutton

info

Q. *What are the state statutory fees?*

A. State statutory fees are guidelines described in law to which the personal representative and the attorney are entitled for the ordinary work involved in a probate.

- Some states set statutory fees as a percentage of the net value of your estate. Other states set statutory fees as a percentage of the gross value of your estate. If fees are based on a percentage of the estate, the attorney and the executor are paid the fee regardless of the number of hours they work.

- Other state statutory fees are described as "reasonable fees." The attorney and the executor are paid for hours they work. **ibutton:** Probate Statutory Fees diesmart.com/ibutton

info

Fact: Allowable statutory fees set by California statute.

California is one of six states where statutory fees are based upon the gross value of your estate. The other forty-four state statutory fees are based upon "reasonable fees" and charged on an hourly basis.

The example below shows the statutory fees a lawyer and an executor have the right to charge. In this case, probate assets consist of a personal residence valued at $1,000,000 and stocks and bonds worth $500,000. Even though there is a $500,000 mortgage, the mortgage does not offset the gross value of the estate subject to state statutory *legal fees. In this instance, allowable probate fees in California can be as much as $67,812.*

Gross Value of Estate	Statutory Allowed Fees	Attorney Fee	Executor Fee	Surety Bond Premium	Court Filing Fees	Combined Fees	% of Estate
$1,500,000	1% of first $100,000	$1,000	$1,000				
	2% of next $100,000	$2,000	$2,000				
	3% of next $800,000	$24,000	$24,000				
	1% of excess	$5,000	$5,000				
		$32,000	**$32,000**	**$300**	**$3,512**	**$67,812**	**4.8%**

Q. *What is a surety bond?*

A. To probate a will, the estate representative may be required to file proof of a bond with the court. The surety bond is that person's promise to act in a responsible manner and to handle the distribution of the estate consistent with all applicable laws.

A person who makes a will may waive the need for bond in his will, and the heirs of a will may also waive bond in writing and then notify the court of the waiver.

ARE YOUR PROBATE RECORDS PUBLIC INFORMATION?

Q. *Why are your probate records public information?*

A. Probate is a public process—it occurs in the courts, and thus the records filed as part of this judicial process are part of the court's records. The contents of your will and other information will be filed as part of the probate process.

These "private documents" are in fact considered public information unless your attorney requests the case and the paperwork to be sealed from the public for a reason the judge finds meaningful.

Most courts or third parties allow anyone to access documents filed with the courts, and some courts make this information available via the Internet. Identity thieves love probate filings.

Some third parties make a business selling financial data they obtain from your probate records. This is how we know the net worth of Elvis Presley and how much money his estate paid for lawyers and taxes.

Fact: The cost and public nature of probate.

When Elvis Presley died, his heirs saw almost 20% of the value of his estate lost to probate fees. Elvis died with only a will. The will had to be filed in probate court. A review of the documents filed after Elvis died reveals the following:

Estate valued at	$10,165,430
Less probate fees	- 1,961,126
Less debts paid	- 3,878,536
Less estate taxes	- 3,339,520
NET TO HEIRS	$966,247

WHEN IS PROBATE REQUIRED?

Q. *How do you know if your estate will require probate?*

A. Your estate representative will need to make an inventory of all your assets. If the estate representative discovers probate assets, the estate is likely subject to probate. As explained earlier, a probate asset is any asset owned by you as an individual and assets where your "estate" is the owner or beneficiary.

Most states have two types of probate procedures: simple and normal. The choice of simple or normal is based upon the combined value of your probate assets and the type of probate asset, i.e. real estate or personal property. Each state has its own laws on what value and what types of probate assets qualify for simple procedures. Each state also sets its own laws on whether the probate value is the fair market value of your assets, or whether the value is the fair market value of your assets less debts you owe when you die.

Most states require the normal process when your probate assets include real estate.

Q. *What happens if the value of your probate assets requires the filing of a normal probate case?*

A. A normal probate process is a court-supervised process. The courts monitor the steps the personal representative takes, adding significant time and costs to the probate process. Furthermore, unless you waive bond in your will, your estate representative may be required to post a bond guaranteeing his or her performance and protecting creditors.

Q. *What happens in a simple probate case?*

A. Some states call a simple probate process a Summary Administration. A judge can have an initial hearing and immediately authorize distribution of the assets to the beneficiaries.

An Affidavit Procedure is available in some states, avoiding a probate hearing. The estate representative or the beneficiary fills out a claim form referred to as an affidavit, stating the owner has died and that he is the new owner of the asset. The new beneficiary sends the affidavit and a copy of the death certificate to the person or entity holding the probate asset (i.e., a brokerage firm or a bank), and requests the probate asset be transferred into the name of the beneficiary.

Fact: Sample of state criteria for simple probate.

State	Maximum Small Estate Value	Property Type
California	$100,000	Real property and personal property
Florida	$ 75,000	Entire estate
New York	$ 20,000	Personal property
Texas	$ 50,000	Entire estate "not including homestead and exempt property"

ibutton: Small Estate Value diesmart.com/ibutton

Q. *How long does probate take?*

A. The probate process proceeds at a rather deliberate pace. The court must ensure proper notice of administration is given to the correct persons; the court must ensure that creditors have had an opportunity to file claims; the personal representative needs time to gather the assets from the estate and have them valued as of the date of death; and the IRS must issue a closing letter regarding estate taxes due.
Until these tasks occur, the probate court will not

authorize final distribution of assets. A relatively uncomplicated probate case can take over a year from filing to closing. During that time, the beneficiaries have neither possession nor control of the property left to them although, in certain circumstances, the beneficiaries may petition the court for a living allowance and/or special funds for things like tuition payments.

Probate takes time because the process is a sequential process, with some time period required before the next step can take place. For instance, the probate process requires sending out a notice to creditors. The court gives the creditors four months to respond. If your estate must file a federal estate tax return, the case will not be closed until the IRS approves the estate tax returns. If the value of your probate assets requires a normal probate procedure, probate could last six to twelve months.

The delay in receiving an inheritance is why heirs receive a direct mail piece offering to loan them money while waiting for inheritance.

A Family Story: Normal probate required.

Britney and Patrick were retired. They had three children, Minnie, Corrie and Christy. Britney and Patrick both had wills. The instructions in their wills gave their share of jointly owned property to the surviving spouse. When the surviving spouse died, the children would each inherit one third of their estate.

Driving home one night, Patrick swerved to avoid a truck and lost control of their car. Both Britney and Patrick died instantly. Britney and Patrick had named their daughter Minnie as executor of their estate. Minnie was a certified financial planner and well versed in various types of financial affairs. After the funeral, Minnie began the process of inventorying her parents' estate. The value of their homes, their oil leases and their brokerage accounts exceeded the small estate limit. Minnie had to use a court-supervised normal probate process to settle her parents' estate.

Minnie hired an attorney specializing in estate law. Minnie explained that Corrie was to begin community college in September. Minnie discovered that before the court could approve the release of any of her parents' money to the beneficiaries she would have to provide an inventory of the assets and a list of the creditors. As part of the probate process, Minnie posted a creditor notice in the newspaper and sent letters notifying creditors of their right to file a claim against the estate. Creditors had four months to respond with any claims against the estate. The money from her parents estate would not be available until the Court was satisfied the estate had the money to pay the creditors and estate taxes.

Corrie had no financial assets of his own. Corrie could miss going to college that fall, unless a petition was made to the court allowing a special preliminary distribution to Corrie for the benefit of his college tuition. Given the debts and relatively low net worth of the estate, it is not certain there would be sufficient assets to allow a court to approve the distribution to Corrie.

CAN YOU AVOID PROBATE WHEN YOU DIE?

Q. *Are there ways to avoid probate?*

A. Yes. Probate is required when you own property as an individual, or when the term "estate" is used to identify an owner or a beneficiary on title and other ownership documents. The way to avoid probate is make sure that property you own is not titled in these manners.

One way to avoid probate is to transfer the title of property you own as an individual to yourself as trustee of a living trust. Although there is some cost in setting up the trust, these costs may be offset by the cost of probate and the cost to your heirs not having access to the estate assets for some period of time.

You may also remove some assets from your probate estate by naming a designated beneficiary on the ownership documents, placing these assets in the automatic inheritance bucket. If you jointly own these assets, each owner may need to sign the beneficiary forms. The designated beneficiary will not inherit the accounts until the last surviving joint tenant dies. The designated beneficiary has no rights to the property until the owner(s) die.

The following assets can have a designated beneficiary named on the ownership documents:

- Checking and Savings Accounts. You can complete a pay-on-death beneficiary form provided by the bank for savings, checking or certificate of deposit accounts.

- Brokerage Accounts: You can complete a transfer-on-death beneficiary form when you complete signature cards.

- Savings Bonds: You can name one designated beneficiary for each savings bond you buy. You can also designate one beneficiary for Treasury bills and Treasury notes.

- Vehicle: Some states also allow you to name a designated beneficiary when you complete your car or boat registration forms: California, Connecticut, Kansas, Missouri and Ohio.

- Real Estate. A transfer-on-death deed allows you to designate a beneficiary when you complete and file a real estate deed. Transfer-on-death deeds are currently only available in these states: Arizona, Colorado, Kansas, Missouri, Nevada, New Mexico and Ohio. **ibutton**: Transfer On Death Forms diesmart.com/ibutton.

A Family Story: Transfer-on-Death deed beneficiary.

Donald and Lorraine lived in Kansas, a state where transfer-on-death deed beneficiaries are available. They owned their house as joint tenants with the right of survivorship.

When talking with their lawyer, the lawyer explained the benefits of making a new transfer-on-death deed naming their two children as beneficiaries.

Their lawyer explained how property owned as joint tenants with the right of survivorship is inherited. When the first spouse dies, the surviving spouse automatically inherits the property. When the last surviving spouse dies, the property is owned by an individual. The property is a probate asset. The couple's children will need some type of document from the probate court before they can sell their house.

Property titled with a transfer-on-death beneficiary deed is different. Donald and Lorraine still own the property in joint tenancy. When the first spouse dies, the surviving spouse automatically inherits the property. However, when the surviving spouse dies, the designated beneficiaries listed on the deed automatically inherit the property. The property is not subject to probate rules and procedures.

Donald and Lorraine completed and filed a transfer-on-death deed naming their children, Angela and Linda, as beneficiaries.

Donald died first. When Lorraine died, Angela and Linda automatically inherited the property. They claimed their inheritance by filing an affidavit with the county recorder stating their parents had died, and attached a copy of a certified death certificate. They are now the legal owners of the property.

Bottom Line:

Property title is just as important as your will. Do it correctly and you can avoid probate. Do it incorrectly and you may accidentally disinherit your beneficiaries.

Action Checklist: Review your property titles and beneficiary forms, and understand what bucket your assets fall into. Take steps to avoid probate.

Find out if there any holes that will cost your family time and money when you die.

- ❑ Find the beneficiary form. Make sure:
  - You have designated a primary and a contingent beneficiary.
  - You have not designated your estate as the beneficiary, unless you wish to do so.
  - You have not named a minor child as a beneficiary without naming a trustee, custodian or guardian for the child.
  - You have changed the names of your designated beneficiaries to reflect changes in your life, such as marriage, divorce, or children.
  - You keep a copy of the documents designating your beneficiaries. Tell someone where you store copies of your beneficiary forms.

- ❑ If you have multiple beneficiaries, confirm what must happen for your beneficiaries to inherit on a per stirpes or per capita basis.

- ❑ If you have divorced, remarried or had children, make sure someone knows where to find your beneficiary forms.

- ❑ Make provisions for simultaneous death. Name a contingent beneficiary. Understand what happens if both you and your primary and/or contingent beneficiary die at the same time.

- ❑ If you want to control the second inheritance of beneficiary assets, talk with an attorney about how to accomplish this goal.

- ❑ If you own property as joint tenants, remember the surviving joint tenant will own the property when you die. They control who inherits the property upon their death.
- ❑ Understand what probate costs in your state.
- ❑ Understand what probate rules are in your state.
- ❑ Determine if you have probate assets.
- ❑ Anticipate the costs and time your estate representative will spend managing your probate assets.
- ❑ Decide if you want to set up a living trust or take other steps to avoid probate.

Mistake #8: You did not know the consequences of adding someone as a joint tenant

Words To Know

- Cost Basis
- Fair Market Value
- Joint Tenant with Right of Survivorship
- Medicaid Penalty Period

A Family Story: Creditor Risk.

Eleanor wanted to make sure her daughter Joy could access her checking account in case something happened to her. Eleanor completed the necessary bank forms and added Joy as a joint tenant. When Eleanor died, Joy would automatically inherit the money in the checking account.

Joy owned a small business. One day Eleanor went to withdraw money from the ATM. A message appeared saying there was no money available.

Eleanor called the bank. The bank explained the Internal Revenue Service had placed a lien on the checking account. Eleanor immediately called Joy. Joy called back later, crying. It appeared Joy's accountant forged documents showing her company had been paying its payroll taxes but, in fact, the payroll taxes had not been paid. Joy, as the owner, is liable for these unpaid payroll taxes. The IRS has the right to place a lien on her mother's joint checking account because Joy is listed as a joint tenant.

WHAT YOU WILL LEARN IN THIS CHAPTER

Married couples routinely own property titled as Joint Tenants with Right of Survivorship. When the first spouse dies, the surviving spouse automatically inherits the property and eliminates the need for probate.

Because the surviving joint tenant wants to avoid probate when they die, the surviving spouse often considers adding one or more of their children to the deed as a method of avoiding probate.

This chapter explains the advantages and disadvantages of adding someone as a joint tenant.

WHAT ARE THE ADVANTAGES OF ADDING SOMEONE AS A JOINT TENANT?

Q. *Why would you add someone as a joint tenant with rights of survivorship ?*

A. The title will automatically and presumptively transfer to the surviving joint tenant without a formal probate procedure.

Many types of property can be owned as joint tenants: bank accounts, brokerage accounts, real estate and vehicles. Parents often see joint tenancy ownership as an easy way to avoid probate and make sure their property is immediately available to their children.

Q. *Does owning property as joint tenants with the right of survivorship provide other benefits when the first joint tenant dies?*

A. Yes. The surviving joint tenant does not have to worry about any creditor claims against the tenant who died. In general, when one joint tenant dies, the only legitimate creditor claims are claims for debts that are the joint responsibility of both joint tenants.

Q. *Is adding your children as joint tenants to a bank or brokerage account or to a U.S. Savings Bond considered a gift?*

A. Yes. The current gift tax allowance is $13,000. If the value of the gift is greater than the annual gift tax allowance, the value of the gift would be included in calculating your $1 million gift tax allowance.

Q. *Is adding your children as joint tenants to a real estate deed considered a gift?*

A. Adding a new joint tenant on a real estate deed is considered a gift because the joint tenant has a present (rather than future) right in the property.

Q. *Who has rights to property you own with someone else while you are living?*

A. You both do, but you must both agree on what to do with the property. Neither one of you can sell titled property like real estate or vehicles, or obtain a loan on the titled property, without the signature of all owners. Either one of you can withdraw all of the money from a checking or savings account. The creditors of one party have the right to the entire value of the property jointly owned.

A Family Story: Joint tenancy disadvantages.

Jodie's mother Genevieve has lived in her family home in Des Moines, Iowa for over fifty years. Genevieve's husband James died last year. Genevieve decided to add Jodie as a joint tenant, knowing Jodie would inherit the property without going through probate.

Jodie had been married to Brian for twenty years. Six months after Genevieve added Jodie's name to the property, Brian decided he wanted a divorce and is now claiming part of the property as his.

WHAT ARE THE DISADVANTAGES OF ADDING SOMEONE AS A JOINT TENANT?

Q. *What should you consider before adding someone as a joint tenant?*

A. There are several things you should consider before adding your children or anyone else as a joint tenant on your property:

- There is no step up in the tax basis of the property when you die. When someone receives a gift, they also receive the cost basis the person giving the gift had.
- You are giving away the opportunity to do tax planning involving that property after you have made someone a joint tenant.
- In some states, the person making the gift may lose homestead or other property tax rights once a joint tenant is added.
- In some states, a divorcing spouse is allowed to make claims against property in which the other spouse has a joint tenancy interest.
- A gift can impact your eligibility for Medicaid.
- Naming someone to jointly own your property is not the same as naming someone to inherit the property when you die. When you add a joint tenant, any action you want to make regarding the property must be agreed to by the joint tenant, including the sale or refinancing of the property.

A Family Story: Gift versus inheritance tax basis.

Pat owned her home for 30 years. She originally purchased the house *for $50,000. For tax purposes, the $50,000 is defined as the cost basis of the property. The term "basis" is the value assigned to property when calculating whether property is sold at a gain or a loss.*

When Pat died, the appraiser determined the fair market value of Pat's house was $350,000

Gift Tax Basis. *Five years before Pat died, Pat added her daughter Barbara as a joint tenant on the real estate deed. The IRS considers this transaction a gift to Barbara.*

When Pat died, Barbara, the surviving joint tenant, automatically inherited the house. Because Barbara was given the property as a gift, Barbara's cost basis will be $50,000, the same cost basis as the person who gave the gift.

Barbara sold the house for $500,000, resulting in a capital gain of $450,000, the difference between the $50,000 cost basis and the $500,000 purchase price. Barbara must report $450,000 of capital gains on her 1040 income tax return and pay any calculated federal and state taxes due.

Inheritance Tax Basis. *If Pat names Barbara as the beneficiary of the house in her will, the tax basis for Barbara changes. Under federal tax law, the basis of inherited property is "stepped-up" to reflect the fair market value at the date of the owner's death. Barbara's cost basis will be the fair market value of her mother's house at the time of inheritance, $350,000. Barbara sells the house she inherited for $500,000. The taxable capital gain is now $150,000.*

Q. *What type of paperwork is required when one of the joint tenants dies?*

A. When the first joint tenant dies, the surviving joint tenant can file a copy of the death certificate with the county recorder or an affidavit of death of joint tenant. Some counties require a new deed be prepared. Other counties just need the death certificate to know one of the joint tenants died.

When the surviving joint tenant dies, some type of probate procedure may be required to transfer the property to the beneficiaries of the surviving joint tenant.

Q. *Can you title property some other way to avoid probate when the last surviving joint tenant dies?*

A. Yes. You can set up a living trust and transfer title of property owned as joint tenants to the trustee of the living trust. Property owned by the trustees of a living trust is not subject to probate.

Bottom Line:

$

Understand the consequences when adding someone else as the owner of your property. It may impact eligibility for Medicaid. When in doubt, consult an attorney.

Action Checklist: Don't add a joint tenant until you understand the consequences.

- ❑ Before adding a spouse or child as a joint tenant to property, carefully consider the consequences of your action.
- ❑ Ask what would happen if a creditor of the new joint tenant put a lien on the asset.
- ❑ Once you add a new joint tenant's name to the ownership documents, you cannot remove it without their approval.
- ❑ The person you name as a joint tenant will automatically inherit the property when you die. It is now theirs. Their estate planning documents will then determine who inherits the property when they die.
- ❑ What if you need to apply for Medicaid within five years from the date you add a joint tenant? How will you pay for long term care during the Medicaid penalty period?

Mistake #9: You failed to maximize the tax deferred value of your IRA, Roth and 401(k) retirement plans

Words to Know:

- 401(k)
- Custodian Agreement
- Converted Roth
- IRA
- IRS Life Expectancy Tables
- Inherited Retirement Accounts
- Keough
- Required Minimum Distribution (RMD)
- Roth 401(k)
- Roth IRA
- SEP
- Stretch IRAs
- Successor Beneficiary

A Family Story: Stretched Roth IRA

Belle named her son Bruce as the beneficiary of her Roth retirement account. The year Belle died, Bruce was 34 years old. The value of the retirement account on December 31st was $100,000.

Bruce elected to set up an inherited retirement account, allowing Bruce to stretch the tax deferred status of his inheritance.

Based upon his age, the IRS Single Life Table sets a life expectancy factor of 48.5 years for Bruce. This means Bruce can stretch the tax deferred distribution of his inherited account for 48.5 years.

Bruce set up an inherited IRA account and named his son Clark as the successor beneficiary. Bruce died 20 years later.

Bruce had used 20 years of his 48.5 year life expectancy factor. Clark, the successor beneficiary, inherits the same life expectancy factor as Bruce. Clark can continue to stretch the tax deferred distributions for another 28.5 years, no matter what age Clark was when Bruce died.

Assuming a rate of return of 8%, the total amount of distributions paid to Bruce and Clark over the 48.5 year period is $1,223,584.

If your retirement account was a Roth account, Bruce and Clark have received $1,223,584 tax free.

The younger the beneficiary is, the greater the life expectancy factor. The IRS Single Life Table establishes a life expectancy factor of 64 years for an 18 year old beneficiary. If an 18 year old beneficiary inherits $100,000 earning an annual rate of return of 8%, the total distributions paid over a 64 year period will be $3,411,195.

An 18 year old beneficiary inheriting $10,000 with a rate of return of 8% a year will receive $341,522 over a period of 64 years.

If the account is an inherited IRA or 401(k), the required minimum distributions would be reported as income on the beneficiary's income tax returns and applicable federal and state taxes would be due. If the account is an inherited Roth account, the distributions are tax free.

WHAT YOU WILL LEARN IN THIS CHAPTER

You and other Americans like you have accumulated an estimated $11 trillion of wealth in retirement plans. That's $2 trillion more than the total market value of all publicly traded U.S. stocks and significantly greater than the $4.5 trillion in total bank deposits reported by the Federal Reserve. Source: Judy Diamond, Journal of Financial Service Professionals, July 2003.

For many of us, individual retirement accounts can be one of our major assets. They include 401(k)s, 403(b)s, Roth Individual Retirement Accounts, self directed Individual Retirement Accounts, Keoghs and SEPs.

We spend a lot of time deciding what to invest in and how to make our 401(k)s and IRAs grow while we are living. Few of us understand the rules and complexities associated with our choices of beneficiaries and their choices when we die. These choices have a huge impact on the long term value of your tax deferred retirement account.

This chapter explains how you and your beneficiaries can maximize the value of your retirement account after you die.

WHAT RULES MANAGE YOUR RETIREMENT ACCOUNTS?

Q. *How do you understand what rules need to be followed when naming a beneficiary and withdrawing money from a retirement account?*

A. The rules regarding the withdrawal and distribution of inherited retirement accounts are complex. If your beneficiaries don't correctly follow the rules in establishing inherited IRAs, the ability to stretch the tax deferred benefits from the account will be lost. If they don't pay any necessary required minimum distributions ("RMDs"), they may be subject to a 50% IRS penalty.

These rules include:

FEDERAL LAWS

Q. *What federal laws manage your retirement account?*

A. Your retirement accounts are your self funded pension. Congress created the rules on how your retirement accounts work. The Internal Revenue Service writes guidelines on how and when to contribute or withdraw distributions in accordance with federal guidelines.

The rules and regulations your beneficiaries must follow for inherited retirement accounts are not managed by your will or living trust. They are governed by a series of complex Internal Revenue Service (IRS) rules dictating the manner and degree to which beneficiaries access the retirement accounts they inherit. Yes, the same IRS which oversees your federal income tax returns.

Think of these retirement account laws as creating a special will directing what happens to your IRA assets. A will you didn't write. A will managed by IRS guidelines and new rulings from the IRS on what the guidelines really mean.

Understanding your beneficiary options and the consequence on the long term tax deferred value of your retirement accounts is essential. If you make a mistake, or your beneficiary makes a mistake, the IRS penalties are harsh and costly.

STATE LAWS

Q. *What state laws manage your retirement account?*

A. Different states have different laws regarding the process necessary if you want to name someone other than your spouse to inherit your retirement accounts. Further, states differ in their treatment of the income generated from IRAs.

CUSTODIAN AGREEMENT

Q. *How does your custodian agreement impact what happens with your retirement account?*

A. When you open a retirement account, you sign a contract with the custodian. Your retirement account is then managed according to the terms of the agreement between you and your custodian. If you are employed and contributing to a 401(k), the custodian is usually your employer. If you have a self directed IRA account at Charles Schwab, Charles Schwab is the custodian.

Although the IRS provides guidelines on how a retirement account should operate, the custodian agreements may be different from one custodian to another. You should read the custodian agreement very carefully.

- You may find the agreement includes language designating a default beneficiary, otherwise known as a "contingent beneficiary", who inherits your retirement account if (a) your designated beneficiaries die before you, (b) you have designated your estate as the beneficiary, or (c) your designated beneficiaries die at the same time you do.
- The agreement may also include default language regarding whether your beneficiaries inherit on a per stirpes or per capita basis. You may find the default provisions don't match your own beneficiary preferences.
- Although new laws permit non-spouse beneficiaries of 401(k) accounts to set up inherited IRAs, not all 401(k) custodian agreements offer this option.

Q. *Why should you consult with someone with specialized retirement knowledge?*

A. We have provided a few questions and answers about naming beneficiaries for retirement accounts and inherited retirement accounts in the charts below.

We highly recommend you, your designated beneficiary, and your executor or trustee visit someone with specialized knowledge about inherited retirement accounts before finalizing your beneficiary choices and before your beneficiaries open up their own inherited retirement accounts. Once a beneficiary has made a choice, the IRS generally does not allow you to go back.

Upon your death, your beneficiary has the choice to immediately withdraw the money or stretch the payout of your retirement account to successor beneficiaries. The longer your retirement account can continue to grow in its tax-deferred status, the bigger its benefits. When making a choice between a 401(k) or a Roth IRA, be sure to consider the after death value to your beneficiaries.

Before finalizing your choice on a Roth IRA versus other choices, or selecting your beneficiaries, visit **ibutton**: Roth IRA www.diesmart.com. You can see the long term value of these accounts based upon the taxable nature of the distributions, your choice of beneficiaries and their life expectancy factor.

WHAT IS THE DIFFERENCE BETWEEN A PRE-TAX RETIREMENT AND A POST-TAX RETIREMENT PLAN?

Q. *What is a pre-tax retirement plan?*

A. 401(k)s, 403(b)s and Individual Retirement Accounts (IRAs) are funded with pre-tax contributions.

- You earn $10,000 in 2011 and you contribute $1,000 to your retirement account.
- You deduct the $1,000 of retirement contributions from your taxable income.

- You report taxable income of $9,000 on your Form 1040 tax return and you pay income taxes on $9,000.

The $1,000 is considered a pre-tax retirement contribution, as you did not pay taxes on the $1,000 contribution you made to your retirement account.

At the age of 70 1/2, you must begin taking distributions from the account, referred to as the Required Minimum Distribution (RMD).

The distributions are reported as ordinary income on your 1040 tax return and any applicable federal and state income taxes must be paid.

Q. *What is a post-tax retirement plan?*

A. Roth IRAs, Roth 401(k) and Roth 403(b) retirement accounts are funded with post-tax contributions.

- You earn $10,000 in 2011 and you contribute $1,000 to your retirement account.

- You report taxable income of $10,000 on your Form 1040 tax return and pay income tax on the entire $10,000.

The $1,000 is considered a post-tax retirement contribution, as you paid taxes on $1,000 of income. Your retirement contributions were made with money you have left after paying any federal and state income taxes due.

You, as the original account owner, are not subject to any required minimum distributions. In fact, the earnings in a post-tax retirement plan may grow tax deferred until you die.

The distributions are not considered as income and no federal income tax is due on the distributions.

CAN YOU DECIDE WHEN YOUR BENEFICIARIES WITHDRAW THE FUNDS THEY INHERIT?

Q. *Who decides when a beneficiary can withdraw funds from an inherited retirement account?*

A. Unless you set up a trust for managing your retirement accounts, your beneficiaries are in control of when they withdraw the funds.

- A beneficiary can immediately withdraw the entire balance of your retirement accounts and pay any taxes due.

- A beneficiary can withdraw the entire amount over a 5 year period and pay any taxes due.

- A beneficiary can set up an inherited IRA account and stretch the tax deferred nature of your accounts.

- A surviving spouse beneficiary can roll over the accounts into his or her own.

WHAT IF YOUR SPOUSE IS YOUR BENEFICIARY?

Q. *Are you required to name your spouse as the beneficiary of your retirement account?*

A. Federal regulations automatically designate your spouse as the beneficiary of your 401(k) or Roth 401(k) retirement account. If you are the account owner of a 401(k) or Roth 401(k), you may not designate another person as the primary beneficiary unless your spouse signs a document approving such a designation. In some cases, the document signed by your spouse must be notarized.

If you live in a community property state, you will also need written spousal consent if you, as the owner of a self directed IRA or Roth IRA, want to designate someone other than your spouse as your primary beneficiary. In some community property states, the document signed by your spouse must be notarized.

If your spouse agrees to naming someone else as beneficiary of your self directed IRA, these states require the consent to be notarized: Alaska, Arizona, California, Idaho, Louisiana, Nevada, New Mexico, Texas, Washington and Wisconsin.

Q. *If you list your spouse as your designated beneficiary, can the surviving spouse roll over your IRA, Roth IRA or 401(k) retirement account into an account of their own?*

A. If your spouse is the only person you name as a beneficiary, your surviving spouse has the right to roll over your retirement account into theirs. Once the roll over is complete, the surviving spouse is listed as the owner of the account. The surviving spouse inherits the same rights as the original owner of the account.

- The surviving spouse can name a designated beneficiary who will inherit the account when the surviving spouse dies.
- The surviving spouse can continue making contributions to the account.
- The assets continue to grow tax deferred.
- A 10% penalty is assessed if the surviving spouse withdraws money before the age of 59 1/2.
- A spouse who inherits an IRA or 401(k) must start taking required minimum distributions (RMD) at the age of 70 1/2 using the IRS Publication 590, Table II life expectancy factor.
- If the account owner who died was taking RMD, the surviving spouse can withdraw funds necessary to pay the required RMD of the deceased without incurring a 10% penalty.
- A spouse who inherits a Roth account can decide when they want to start taking withdrawals.

Only a spouse can elect to roll over the original account owner's IRA into his or her own account. All other IRA beneficiaries must establish inherited IRA accounts. The spouse beneficiary must withdraw the assets from the decedent's retirement account and deposit them into their own IRA account within 60 days.

- If you request the existing financial organization to move the decedent's account directly to the financial institution where the new account is being established, the transfer is not a taxable event.

- If you withdraw the money and do not complete the transfer within 60 days, the withdrawal becomes a taxable event.

If a surviving spouse is not the sole beneficiary, the surviving spouse and the other named beneficiaries must set up inherited accounts.

Q. *Can a surviving spouse elect to stay a beneficiary?*

A. Yes. A surviving spouse has the right to stay a beneficiary rather than rolling over your retirement account into theirs. If they elect to do this, they must set up an inherited retirement account and will have the same rights as all beneficiaries of an inherited retirement account.

Some surviving spouses may find a beneficiary choice is better if they need to take distributions before they reach the age of 59 1/2 without paying a 10% early withdrawal penalty.

The downside of an inherited IRA versus a rollover is the surviving spouse beneficiaries are treated as successor beneficiaries. Their life expectancy factor is inherited from the life expectancy of the surviving spouse, reducing the ability of a young beneficiary to stretch the payout over a long period of time.

WHAT IF SOMEONE OTHER THAN YOUR SPOUSE IS THE NAMED BENEFICIARY?

Q. *What options does a beneficiary other than a spouse have when they inherit a retirement account?*

A. A beneficiary can elect to immediately withdraw all of the money, or the beneficiary can elect to set up an inherited retirement account.

Q. *What is an inherited retirement account?*

A. An inherited retirement account allows your spouse and any other designated beneficiary to maintain the tax deferred nature of your account. The length of time the funds can continue to grow tax deferred depends upon the beneficiary's age when he or she inherited the account. Some people refer to this as "stretching" the retirement account.

No matter whether the original retirement account is a 401(k), a self-directed IRA or a Roth IRA, beneficiaries other than a spouse can only set up inherited accounts. Although the original owner of a Roth IRA is not subject to required minimum distribution calculations, their beneficiaries are.

Q. *Can a beneficiary of a company sponsored retirement account set up an inherited retirement account?*

A. The rules are different for company sponsored retirement plans and self directed IRAs and Roth accounts.

Until the Pension Reform Act of 2006 was passed, non-spouse beneficiaries of 401(k) (and other company sponsored retirement plans) were not allowed to set up inherited IRAs. Previously, only a spouse had this right. All other non-spouse beneficiaries had to comply with the company plan rules, which usually required an immediate distribution of the retirement funds, or allowed the funds to be distributed in a one or two year window.

A non-spouse beneficiary immediately saw the value of his or her inheritance disappear as the beneficiary would have to pay income taxes on the withdrawal of the funds. Under the new Pension Reform Act rules, the non-spouse beneficiary can now roll over the funds into an inherited account. This right for a non-spouse beneficiary to roll over a 401(k) account is not a mandatory requirement. The custodian agreement governing the 401(k) plan you are part of must offer this feature.

Q. *Can a beneficiary of a self directed retirement account set up an inherited retirement account?*

A. A spouse has the option to set up an inherited IRA account. Anyone other than a spouse must set up an inherited IRA account if they want to continue the tax deferred value of the account.

Not all custodian agreements provide the option for your beneficiaries to set up their own inherited IRAs. If the option is not present, the beneficiary has the right to change custodians. If the beneficiary elects to not change custodians, the beneficiary must immediately withdraw all of the funds from your account, report the withdrawal as ordinary income on their 1040 tax return and pay any federal or state taxes due.

WHAT SHOULD YOU KNOW ABOUT INHERITED RETIREMENT ACCOUNTS?

Q. *How do you set up an inherited retirement account??*

A. The rules for setting up inherited retirement accounts are the same, no matter whether the original account was an 401(k)/IRA or a Roth 401(k)/Roth IRA retirement plan. Make sure you understand the rules for inherited IRAs; otherwise you may lose the ability to stretch the value of the retirement account.

- The name of the original retirement account owner continues to be listed as the owner on the inherited account paperwork.

- The social security number of the beneficiary inheriting the account is added to the account records. All distributions will be reported to the IRS using the beneficiary's SSN.

- A beneficiary of an inherited account cannot make further contributions to the account

- There is no 10% penalty for taking distributions before the age of 59 1/2.

- If there are multiple beneficiaries, a separate account must be established for each beneficiary by December 31 of the calendar year following your year of death.

401(k) and other company sponsored retirement accounts have an additional rule for inherited IRAs:

- The distribution must take place after January 1, 2007.

- The transfer must go directly from your 401(k) account to the inherited beneficiary account. The check must be made payable to the name of the inherited account, not the name of the beneficiary.

Q. *How does a beneficiary calculate their required minimum distributions (RMD)?*

A. The beneficiary should first determine the life expectancy factor for their age in the year after the retirement account owner's death. Life expectancy factors are specified by the IRS and can be found in IRS Publication 590, Table 1.

Next, the beneficiary should determine the balance of the inherited IRA as of December 31 of the preceding year.

Divide the account balance by the life expectancy factor. This will be the required minimum distribution (RMD) the first year.

For subsequent years, you do not need to look up a new life expectancy factor. Just reduce the life expectancy factor number by one for each year.

A Family Story: Calculating the RMD.

Keith, the account owner, died in 2007. Keith named Isabella, his daughter, the designated beneficiary. In 2007, Isabella was 50 years old. The balance of Keith's account December 31, 2007 was $200,000.

In 2008, Isabella calculated her required minimum distribution. In 2008, the year after the account owner died, Isabella was 51. Isabella looked up her life expectancy factor in Publication 590, IRS Table 1 and found it was 33.3 years.

Isabella calculated the RMD by dividing the balance in the retirement account as of December 31, 2007 ($200,000) by a life expectancy factor of 33.3 years. Isabella must take a required minimum distribution of $6,006 in 2008.
Isabella's life expectancy factor will be reduced by one each year thereafter. In 2009, Isabella will calculate the RMD by dividing the value of the inherited retirement account on December 31, 2008 by a life expectancy factor of 32.3 years.

Q. *What happens if your designated beneficiary dies before all of the inherited retirement funds are distributed?*

A. When the designated beneficiary of the original account owner sets up his or her inherited retirement account, IRS regulations allow the designated beneficiary to name a successor beneficiary.

If the beneficiary of the inherited IRA dies and funds are still available for distribution, a named living successor beneficiary can continue to take advantage of the stretch payout available to the original designated beneficiary. The successor beneficiary uses the life expectancy factor of the original beneficiary when determining their RMDs. The successor beneficiary has the same rights as the original beneficiary. The successor beneficiary can name their own successor beneficiary, who will inherit the funds if the funds from the original account have not been distributed. The account balance continues to grow on a tax deferred basis.

The industry refers to this opportunity to name beneficiaries and their ability to name successor beneficiaries as a "stretched" IRA.

Q. *Can an inherited IRA be changed from its original designation as an IRA to a Roth IRA?*

A. Funds in an inherited IRA are not eligible to be converted to a Roth IRA. You, the original account owner, would need to convert an IRA or a 401(k) to a Roth IRA or a Roth 401(k) before you die if you want your children or grandchildren to receive tax free distributions from an inherited retirement account. If you are considering a Roth conversion, don't forget to include the tax free benefits a stretch IRA could provide your children and grandchildren

Q. *Will your beneficiaries need to pay income tax on their withdrawals?*

A. The beneficiary of an inherited retirement account assumes the same income tax rules as the original account owner. The income tax rules are applicable whether the beneficiary immediately withdraws all of the retirement funds or whether he receives income from a stretched inherited retirement account.

The custodian of an inherited account will mail IRS Form 1099-R to the beneficiary reporting the total amount of distributions. The beneficiary will report 1099-R income on his or her 1040 tax return and pay the applicable tax for the entire tax return. State taxes may also be due.

The beneficiaries of a post-tax inherited retirement account, Roth IRAs and Roth 401(k)s, receive their distributions tax free.

Q. *Does the income from a retirement account impact Social Security benefits?*

A. Some part of your Social Security benefits may be taxable if your income exceeds certain levels. The IRS counts half your Social Security benefit, income from pensions, investment earnings and withdrawals from regular 401(k)s and IRAs.

Withdrawals from Roth accounts are excluded from this calculation, which may increase the value of your Social Security benefits.

Q. *What if your estate is subject to estate tax?*

A. If your estate pays an estate tax, your beneficiaries can offset some of the income using an obscure tax deduction known as the "Income In Respect of a Decedent". See your accountant for more information.

Q. *What if the Roth retirement account is less than 5 years old?*

A. Roth IRAs and Roth 401(k) retirement accounts have a five year window rule impacting what taxes are on contributions.

If you inherit a Roth retirement account in 2011 that was established in 2009, you must separate the funds in the account between contributed funds and earnings.

If the Roth retirement account includes $100,000 of funds from a rollover contribution and $8,000 of earnings, the beneficiary can immediately withdraw the entire $108,000. You will not owe taxes on the $100,000 of contributed funds, but you must report the $8,000 as income on your 1040 tax return and pay applicable taxes.

You can also elect to withdraw the $100,000 and pay no tax or penalty and leave the $8,000 of earnings to grow tax free until 20114 Once the five year window passes, you can withdraw the balance of the Roth retirement account tax free.

Fact: 401(k) pre-tax credits.

If you contributed both pre-tax and after-tax dollars to your 401(k) or IRA retirement accounts, leave documentation for your beneficiaries.

Your beneficiary will need to know this when they prepare their 1040. Any after-tax dollars can be allocated and no income taxes will be due on the percentage of income allocated to after-tax contributions.
The fact that your beneficiaries inherit the same tax status as the original owner can have a huge impact on the long term value of 401(k)s and IRAs versus a Roth retirement account.

Look at this example:

		Roth IRA or Roth 401(k)	IRA or 401(k)
Value When Original Account Owner Dies		$100,000	$100,000
Beneficiary Age		35	35
Life Expectancy Factor		48.5	48.5
Annual Appreciation Rate		8%	8%
Total amount of RMD over 48.5 years		$1,223,584	$1,223,584
Beneficiary Federal Income Tax Rate		35%	35%
Income Taxes Due		$0	$428,254
Net to Beneficiary		$1,223,584	$795,330

Q. *What if the original owner of a 401(k) or IRA account dies before he is required to begin taking required minimum distributions?*

A. If the original account owner of a 401(k) or IRA account dies under the age of 70 1/2 and has not started taking required minimum distributions, the named beneficiary of the inherited account has the option to (a) withdraw all of the funds in the retirement account before the end of the fifth year after the account owner's death without any 10% penalty for early withdrawal; or (b) to open up an inherited retirement account described above.

The beneficiary must make this election by the end of the first year (December 31) after your death and inform the custodian of their choice. If they don't, the IRS takes the position that the beneficiary must be treated as if you named your "estate" as the beneficiary.

If the original account owner dies over the age of 70 1/2 and has started taking required minimum distributions, the designated named beneficiary may only elect option b.

Q. *What are the distribution rules when you name multiple beneficiaries for your inherited retirement account?*

A. The beneficiaries have the right to split your retirement account into separate accounts. If they do so, the life expectancy factor will be that of each individual beneficiary who set up an inherited account. The split must be done by September 30th following the year of your death.

If the beneficiaries don't split the account into separate accounts, the life expectancy factor for all the beneficiaries will be the same and will be calculated based upon the age of the oldest beneficiary.

Fact: Named beneficiary is a trust or a charity.

If you intend to name a charity or a trust as one of your beneficiaries of a retirement account, make sure someone with inherited retirement account expertise assists you in this regard. The naming of a charity or trust may affect the ability of your other beneficiaries to stretch the payouts based upon their own life expectancies.

Q. *What happens if your estate is listed as the beneficiary or the estate becomes the default beneficiary?*

A. Naming your estate as the beneficiary of your IRA,

or having the estate become the beneficiary because there is no living named beneficiary, has a variety of consequences.

A named beneficiary has an immediate right to distribute the retirement assets upon your death. When the beneficiary is the estate, the account is a probate asset and will be subject to the same delays, costs and processes as other assets that are being probated.

Most custodial agreements provide that if an owner dies without naming a beneficiary of their account, the account beneficiary is the owner's estate. In such a case, the account beneficiaries will be the heirs of your estate determined by your will or, if you don't have a will, state intestate statutes. However, some IRA custodial agreements contain language that in the absence of a named beneficiary, upon the owner's death the account money belongs to a spouse, then to surviving children, before the estate becomes the beneficiary.

The beneficiaries determined by a will (or laws of intestate succession) lose their right to "stretch" the payout of the retirement account. They must either withdraw all of the funds within five years or use the life expectancy factor of the original owner of the retirement account.

If the beneficiary of a traditional IRA is determined by a will or intestate succession laws, these rules apply:

- If the deceased original owner of the account was over the age of 70 1/2 and was already taking required minimum distributions, the beneficiary determined by the owner's will (or state intestate succession laws) assumes the life expectancy factor of the original owner based on the IRS Single Life Expectancy Table. If the owner dies at the age of 80, the new beneficiary inherits a life expectancy factor of 10. The beneficiary must withdraw all of the money within 10 years of the year of the original owner's death.

- If the deceased original owner was under the age of 70 1/2 and was not taking required minimum distributions, the new designated beneficiary must withdraw all of the funds by the end of the fifth year following the year of the owner's death. No distribution is required for any year before that fifth year.

A Family Story: Estate as IRA beneficiary.

Ross died in 2006 at the age of 80. Ross was taking required minimum distributions from his IRA. Ross had named his estate as the beneficiary for his IRA. The account balance on December 31, 2006 was $100,000.

Since there was no designated beneficiary, the retirement account is a probate asset. The beneficiaries will be determined by Ross's will or, if there is no will, by state intestate secession laws.

Based on instructions in Ross's will, his son Greg inherited his IRA. Greg was only 40 years old when his father died. Because Greg was not a designated beneficiary, Greg is not able to use his own life expectancy factor. Instead, Greg must use the life expectancy of his father.

In 2007, Ross would have been 81 years old. His life expectancy factor is 9.2 years. Greg must take a required minimum distribution of $10,870 ($100,000 divided by 9.2), the first year and must withdraw all of the funds over the next 9.2 years.

If Ross had died in 2006, and had not yet begun taking required minimum distributions, Greg would need to withdraw all of the funds in the retirement account within 5 years.

Q. *What happens if you name a minor child as a beneficiary?*

A. Minor children cannot inherit money or other

property until they are legally an adult, which happens when they turn 18 or 21, depending on state laws.

An owner may name an IRA trust for the benefit of their minor child as a beneficiary and/or an owner may name a custodian as the designated beneficiary for the benefit of a minor child. Rather than listing a child, Jane Doe, as a beneficiary on a beneficiary form, you can list the custodian for the beneficiary, e.g., John Doe, as custodian for Jane Doe.

As the custodian, John will be responsible for taking the required minimum distributions and depositing them in a bank account. When Jane becomes an adult, she becomes responsible for taking required minimum distribution or electing to withdraw all of funds remaining in the retirement account.

Q. *What happens if a trust is listed as the designated beneficiary?*

A. If you wish to name a trust to be the beneficiary of a retirement account, you should consult with a knowledgeable tax planner and/or attorney. The trust provisions must have special language needed to identify the beneficiaries of your inherited account and qualify the trust as a look through trust. If certain language is not present, the beneficiaries may likely lose their ability to stretch the payout.

The trustee should request the IRA custodian to complete new forms for an inherited IRA. The name of the owner remains the original owner, but the documents now identify the trust as the entity to receive the distributions and IRS Form 1099. Naming your trust as a beneficiary means the custodian will pay the distributions to your trust. The trust will then pay the beneficiaries income received from the IRA.

Naming a trust as the beneficiary is not the same as transferring your retirement account into the name of the trust. By transferring the account to the name of the trust, the account may lose the its tax-deferred status.

WHY WOULD YOU ESTABLISH A TRUST AS THE BENEFICIARY OF YOUR RETIREMENT ACCOUNT?

Q. *What are the advantages of naming a trust as your beneficiary?*

A. Naming an IRA trust as the beneficiary of your retirement accounts provides you with several options not available if you name an individual as the designated beneficiary.

- You can control when a beneficiary can withdraw the funds. If you want to maximize the value of a stretched IRA, consider setting up an IRA trust.

  The instructions in the trust will provide that the distribution of income from your IRA to the beneficiaries will be stretched. The beneficiaries cannot immediately cash out the account, which is then held in trust. If you just name an individual as the beneficiary, that individual can elect whether to immediately cash out the account or set up an inherited account.

- If the beneficiary is a minor child, the trustee can name a custodian who will manage the money on behalf of the minor child.

- You may want to control the second inheritance of the account. If you are in a second marriage, you may want to give your spouse distributions from an inherited retirement account while he or she is living, but control who inherits the accounts when he or she dies. In contrast, if you name your spouse as the primary beneficiary, the spouse will also inherit the right to determine who receives distributions when he or she dies.

Be sure and consult an attorney with knowledge in this area. The IRA trust needs special language identifying the beneficiaries. If the IRS does not believe the trust meets its requirement for naming beneficiaries, the trustee must take a lump sum distribution of the assets or pay out all of the funds within a five year period.

ARE RETIREMENT ACCOUNTS PART OF YOUR TAXABLE ESTATE?

Q. *Are retirement accounts subject to estate tax?*

A. Yes. No matter what type of retirement account you own, the account balance is included as part of your taxable estate. The funds in your Roth IRA are part of your taxable estate even though your distributions from a Roth IRA are tax free.

Q. *What happens if a prenuptial agreement regarding a spouse right to a retirement account is signed before you marry?*

A. The Employee Retirement Income Security Act (ERISA) of 1974 protects the pension rights of spouses to 401(k) accounts. In order for a spouse to forfeit those spousal pension rights under ERISA, they would have to consent to waive those rights.

.

If the terms of a prenuptial agreement include spousal rights to a 401(k), make sure the new spouse signs this prenuptial agreement AFTER you marry.

ERISA has ruled that a prenuptial agreement waiving spousal pension rights is not valid, because only a spouse can waive pension rights on a company plan. A prenuptial agreement isn't signed by a spouse, it is signed by a fiance who isn't a spouse even if the agreement is signed one second before the wedding.

ERISA clearly states only a spouse can waive these rights, not a non-spouse. Include language in the prenuptial agreement whereby the fiancee agrees to sign a valid spousal waiver as soon as the fiancee becomes a spouse.

If you live in a community property state, similar laws apply to IRA accounts.

Bottom Line:

Consider setting up Roth accounts for you, your children and your grandchildren.

This can be a great way to save money for your children and your grandchildren, and provide a tax free income stream during your lifetime or after your death.

Action Checklist: Maximize the value of your tax deferred retirement accounts.

- ☐ Read the custodial document provided by the company managing your retirement accounts.
- ☐ Make sure you understand if there are any default clauses determining who will inherit your account if you name your estate as the beneficiary.
- ☐ Ask if there are any default clauses determining who inherits the retirement account if all of your named beneficiaries die before you do or at the same time you do.
- ☐ If you name a minor child as a primary or contingent beneficiary, ask how you designate a custodian to manage the money on behalf of a minor child.
- ☐ If you have named multiple beneficiaries, decide whether you want these beneficiaries to inherit per stirpes or per capita. Make sure the custodial agreement and the way you listed your beneficiaries meet your wishes.
- ☐ If you need to customize your beneficiary designation form, make sure it is acceptable by the custodian. Request a signed receipt confirming their receipt of your beneficiary form. Make sure your estate representative has a copy of this beneficiary form.

- ❑ If you are in a second marriage, pay special attention when you designate your beneficiaries. If a second spouse has waived their spousal rights, make sure the documents are signed when he or she is a spouse, not a finance.

- ❑ Consider naming both a primary and a contingent beneficiary.

- ❑ Play "what if" with your choice of beneficiaries and see if your choice of beneficiaries optimizes the tax deferred value of your retirement accounts. **ibutton:** Inherited IRA Calculator www.diesmart.com.

- ❑ Consult with a professional experienced with IRAs. Ask him or her to review your choice of beneficiaries and your custodian agreement to see if both meet your wishes.

info

- ❑ Consider setting up an IRA trust if you want to keep your beneficiaries from immediately withdrawing all of the funds and losing the value of its tax deferred status.

- ❑ If your children or grandchildren work while in school, consider setting up a Roth account for them.

- ❑ If you participate in a 401(k) and you purchased company stock using your 401(k) funds, find out more about what tax professionals refer to as net unrealized appreciation (NUA). The NUA provides a special tax treatment on the appreciation of the stock which may impact whether your beneficiaries elect a lump sum distribution, a roll over or set up an inherited account.

Mistake #10: You did not understand minor children can be a major problem

Words to Know:

- Custodian
- Education Savings Account (ESA)
- Guardian
- Guardian of the Estate
- Guardian of the Person
- Guardianship
- Minor
- Pet Sanctuary
- Pet Trust

A Family Story: Courts supervise the assets of a minor.

If you aren't a teenager, the web site whateverlife.com may not be familiar to you. According to Google Analytics, whateverlife.com attracts more than 7 million individuals and 60 million page views a month. That's a larger audience than the circulations of Seventeen, Teen Vogue and CosmoGirl! magazines combined. Quantcast, a popular source among advertisers, ranked whateverlife.com No. 349 in July, 2007 out of more than 20 million sites. Among the sites in its rearview mirror: Britannica.com, AmericanIdol.com, FDA.gov and CBS.com.

The entrepreneur responsible for the success of whateverlife is Ashley Qualls, who started the company when she was 14. Running a growing company without an MBA, not to mention a high-school diploma, is hard enough but Ashley confronted another extraordinary complication.

Business associates may forget that she is 17, but Detroit's Wayne County Probate Court has not. She's a minor with considerable assets--"business affairs that may be jeopardized," the law reads--that need protection in light of the rift her sudden success has caused in an already fractious family. In January, a probate judge ruled that neither Ashley nor her parents could adequately manage her finances. Until she turns 18 next June, a court-appointed conservator is controlling whateverlife's assets; Ashley must request funds for any expense outside the agreed upon monthly budget. Any joint venture Ashley wants to enter into must be approved by the probate court.

The arrangement, she says, affects her ability to react in a volatile industry. "It's not like I'm selling lemonade." Besides, it's her company. If she wants to contract developers or employ her mother, why shouldn't she be able to do it without the conservator's approval?

Ashley has hired a lawyer to emancipate herself and be declared an adult. Now. At 17.

WHAT YOU WILL LEARN IN THIS CHAPTER

Parents have the right to appoint someone to be responsible for the daily care of their children, commonly called the guardian of the person.

Parents, grandparents and others have the right to give property to a minor child. Individuals routinely name a minor child as a beneficiary on beneficiary forms or in their wills without understanding the consequences.

By law, minor children cannot own property outright. Asssets given to a minor child must be managed by an adult. Naming a minor child as a designated beneficiary on a beneficiary form or in your will usually means the probate courts must become involved in the management of their inheritance until the child becomes an adult. In addition, giving money directly to a child with "special needs" may impact their ability to receive government benefits.

Most states define minors as persons under the age of eighteen; some states define minors as persons under the age of twenty-one. **ibutton:** Minor Child Age Rules diesmart.com/ibutton

This chapter explains the three ways of giving money for the benefit of a minor child. The method you choose determines whether the probate court is involved in the management of their inheritance and the age the minor child gains control of their inheritance.

WHO DO YOU WANT TO MANAGE YOUR CHILDREN'S DAILY CARE WHEN YOU DIE?

Q. *What is a guardian of the person?*

A. You have the right to nominate a guardian of the person to take care of your children.

The guardian of the person has day-to-day responsibility for your children, assuming the role of a substitute parent. When you die, someone must petition the court to be appointed as the guardian of the person. The court will normally defer to the person you nominate as the guardian of the person. Other individuals have the right to petition the court to serve in these roles. If this should happen, the court will examine who best will protect the interests of the minor(s) and appoint that person as the guardian of the person.

If you don't nominate a guardian of the person, the court will do it for you, according to state rules of preferences. A surviving parent usually comes first, followed by grandparents if neither parent is alive.

Fact: Surviving parent rights.

If one parent dies, the surviving parent continues to have the right to take personal care of minor children.

When a divorced or single parent dies, the court generally appoints the surviving parent as guardian of the person for a minor or disabled child, even if the deceased parent would have been opposed to that.

WHO DO YOU WANT TO MANAGE YOUR MONEY ON BEHALF OF A MINOR CHILD?

AT WHAT AGE DO YOU WANT YOUR CHILDREN TO HAVE ACCESS TO THE MONEY?

Q. *What should you know about giving money to minor children?*

A. There are several choices available for giving

property to a minor child. You can set up a trust. You can name a custodian. Or, you can nominate a guardian of the estate in your will.

These choices impact the age at which a minor child will inherit the property, who is in charge of the property until that time, and, the involvement of the probate court.

CHOICE #1: TRUSTS FOR CHILDREN

Q. *What if you set up a child's trust?*

A. You can include instructions in your living trust or a testamentary trust in your will establishing a new trust for your minor or disabled children when you die.

- You can specify what assets you want transferred to the trust to be used for the benefit of your minor or disabled children.
- You can name the trustee you want to manage these assets for your children, either an individual or a financial institution.
- There is no requirement for the probate courts to be involved in the handling of a trust for your child.
- Unlike state laws which give inherited probate property to minors when they reach age 18, your trust can include instructions about the age at which you want the children to inherit the property, e.g., one half at age 25 and the remainder at age 35.

If you become mentally incompetent, your living trust can give the trustee the right to manage trust assets for your minor or disabled children.

CHOICE #2: CUSTODIANSHIP

A law known as the Uniform Transfers to Minors Act (UTMA) allows you to name an adult custodian to manage specific accounts that will be held for the benefit of a minor child until the minor child is considered an adult. You can name a custodian in your will, your living trust or on beneficiary forms.

- No court process is required to approve the custodian. No court supervision of the custodian is required.
- State law determines what property can be owned in a custodial account.

Q. *How do you designate a custodian on beneficiary forms?*

A. If you want "John Jones," your minor child, to get the proceeds of a life insurance policy, you would fill out the beneficiary designation like this: "Mike Smith, as custodian for John Jones under the Uniform Transfers to Minors Act." If you die or become incapacitated before John becomes an adult, Mike, the designated custodian, manages the account until John reaches the age at which state law considers him to be an adult.

Q. *How do you designate a custodian in your will?*

A. If you want "Allison Astor," a minor child, to be a beneficiary in your will, you would fill out the beneficiary instructions like this: "All property I leave by my will to Allison Astor shall be given to her mother, Kim Astor, as custodian for Allison Astor under the Uniform Transfer to Minors Act of California."

Fact: Uniform Transfers to Minors Act.

fyi

The Uniform Transfers to Minors Act has replaced the Uniform Gifts to Minors Act (UGMA) in many states, allowing nearly all types of property, including real estate, to be held in such an account.

All states except Vermont and South Carolina have adopted UTMA law, which superseded UGMA law.

Q. *Can you designate yourself as a custodian on accounts while you are living?*

A. You can set up banking accounts, checking accounts or brokerage accounts for a minor child or grandchild while you are living. Since a minor child can't own and manage these accounts, you may designate yourself as the custodian of these accounts.

If you are considering setting up a custodial account while you are living, consider these facts:

- Once you have deposited money into a checking account or bought stock in a brokerage account under the UTMA, the money or the stock belongs to the child. You can't take it back.
- When the child is considered an adult by state law, (age 18 or 21, depending on the state), the custodian must give the control of the assets to the minor child. If there are significant assets, think about what someone who is 18 or 21 will do with them.
- If your child dies before he or she becomes an adult, the assets will pass according to the UTMA laws of your state. The beneficiaries may not be the ones you would have selected.
  info **ibutton:** UTMA property rules diesmart.com/ibutton
- When the child applies for financial aid for college, assets owned by them will affect their eligibility for financial aid.

- A custodial account can be used to manage the assets only for one child. You can't transfer assets from one child's account to another.
- If you name yourself as the custodian and you die before the child becomes an adult, the custodial account will be included as part of your taxable estate. This is true even though the transfers to the account are completed gifts. The account is included in your estate because you retained the power to determine how your gift would be applied for the benefit of the child. You perhaps could avoid the problem by naming as custodian someone who will not make any gifts to the account. For example, a grandparent might name the parent as the custodian.

CHOICE #3: GUARDIAN OF THE ESTATE DESIGNATED IN YOUR WILL

Q. *How do you appoint someone to manage property on behalf of a minor child in your will?*

A. If you have a will, you have the right to nominate a person or a financial institution as the guardian of the estate for your minor or disabled children. When you die, the guardian will file papers with the court requesting approval of your nominee. Once appointed by the courts, the guardian of the estate will assume financial control of the child's bequest and manage it for the benefit of the child.

- Most courts require the guardian of the estate to purchase a surety bond as part of the guardianship process.

- Most state laws terminate the guardianship of the estate when the minor becomes a legal adult (turns 18 or 21), at which time the funds are given over to the child.

- The guardian of the estate will be required to file annual reports with the courts, which become public records and are available for public access. The actions of the guardian may be subject to court review and may restrict how the guardian can use the funds for the benefit of a minor child.

Q. *What are the other disadvantages of using a will to name a guardian of the estate for a minor child?*

A. When you name a minor child as a beneficiary, some states set limits on the amount of money a guardian of the estate can manage on behalf of a minor child. If the amount of inheritance exceeds state limits, some states require a separate court procedure called a Conservatorship. The conservator will be required to report on a regular basis how he manages and spends the child's inheritance. For a fee.

The court appointed conservator becomes responsible for deciding how to invest and spend the money on behalf of a minor child, not the guardian you named. Their choices may be dictated by state statutes.

Using California as an example:

- If a minor inherits $5K or less, his parent may hold the inheritance money and /or property in trust for the benefit of the minor until he or she reaches the age of 18.

- If the minor inherits more than $5K but not more than $20K, the court has discretion to hold the money on any condition it determines to be in the best interest of the minor.

- If a minor inherits more than $20K, the court may:

    - Order a guardian of the estate to be appointed so that the money is deposited with the guardian.

    - Order the money to be deposited in an insured account.

- Order the money to be transferred in whole or in part to a custodian account in compliance with the California Uniform Transfers to Minor Account and order the money to be deposited with the county treasurer. **ibutton:** Minor child inheritance rules diesmart.com/ibutton

If you don't make a will, the probate court will appoint a guardian of the estate for your minor children.

HOW SHOULD YOU PLAN FOR CHILDREN WITH SPECIAL NEEDS?

Q. *What if you have a child with special needs?*

A. Consider a type of trust referred to as a special needs trust. A special needs trust is a trust that provides for children with special needs but does not cause them to become ineligible for certain government benefits such as SSI and Medicaid. The laws concerning eligibility are complex and changing. Because of this, you should seek the help of a competent lawyer.

WHO WILL TAKE CARE OF YOUR CHILDREN IF YOU BECOME INCAPACITATED?

Q. *How do you document your wishes regarding the guardian of the person?*

A. Your will is not considered a legal document until you die. Even though you named a guardian of the person in your will, you should prepare a form nominating a guardian of the person in the event you become incapacitated.

There is no specific form you use to nominate someone to be the guardian of the person. You can write your wishes on a plain piece of paper and sign the document before a notary.

ibutton: Guardian Nomination Form diesmart.com/ibutton

Q. *Who will manage your money on behalf of your minor child?*

A. If you have a living trust, the trust can include instructions on using trust assets to take care of minor children.

Your durable power of attorney can give your financial agent the right to manage financial assets on behalf or your minor children.

WHAT ARE SECTION 529 AND COVERDELL SAVINGS PLANS?

Q. *How can a Coverdell account or Section 529 account be used to manage money on behalf of a minor child?*

A. Section 529 accounts and Coverdell accounts are another way to give money for the benefit of a minor child.

Parents, grandparents, or aunts and uncles can open a 529 or a Coverdell account and name a minor child as the beneficiary of the account.

The account owner can contribute money to the savings account each year. The funds in the account will grow tax free. The beneficiary can withdraw the money in a tax free manner to pay for qualified educational expenses.

- Anyone can contribute $13,000 per year free from gift tax to a 529 account. Once money is given to a 529 plan, the managers of the 529 plan make investment choices regarding the funds in the plan.
- Individuals meeting income qualifications can contribute $2,000 per year per beneficiary to a Coverdell account. The owner of the account determines how to manage and invest the money.

The money the account owner transfers into the 529 account or the Coverdell account is used to save for the beneficiary's educational expenses.

The rules and regulations of both 529 plans and Coverdell accounts are managed by federal laws. If the account owner dies before all funds are distributed to the beneficiary, a successor owner can be named to manage the account. Section 529 accounts and Coverdell Savings accounts are generally not considered part of the account owner's taxable estate.

If the beneficiary dies before the funds are spent, the account owner can usually change the name of the beneficiary to another qualified beneficiary.

See a qualified financial planner to find out how these accounts can be used to give money for the benefit of a minor child.

Fact:
Donated sperm or eggs.

Reproductive medicine has produced many new challenges for courts and legislatures. One such challenge concerns the inheritance rights of children born after the death of a genetic parent. In earlier times, laws governing posthumous reproduction had to consider only children born within nine months of a biological father's death. Today, however, cryopreservation of sperm and embryos makes it possible for children to be born years after the death of a genetic father or mother.
If you have been part of an artificial reproduction program, leave clear guidelines on what you want done with any donated eggs or sperm.

WHAT IF YOU THINK OF YOUR PETS AS YOUR CHILDREN?

Q. *How can you make sure your pets will be cared for?*

A. If you love your pets, plan for their existence after you are gone. An estimated 500,000 pets are euthanized each year because no plans were made for them in the event of their owner's death or long-term illness.

You generally cannot make a gift of money or other property to a pet in a will or living trust. The law considers a pet to be property and one piece of property cannot hold title to another piece of property. Language giving gifts directly to pets is not going to be enforced by the courts.

What you can do is designate someone you trust to take responsibility for your pets when you die or if you become so disabled you can't care for them. You can also give money, either outright or in trust, to this person. Although the money is to be used for the care of your pets, the courts have no way to enforce these terms if you simply give the money outright.

Q. *What is a Pet Trust?*

A. Some states have trust laws which allow a trust to be set up for "the care of a designated domestic or pet animal." The trustee is prohibited from using any of the principal or income of the trust for anything other than the welfare of the designated animal. Just as important, state laws have made the terms of the trust enforceable.

The pet owner can designate a person with the power to enforce the trust, that is, to make certain the trustee is using the principal and income for the benefit of the pet. If the pet owner does not name a trust enforcer, any individual may ask the court to appoint a trust enforcer. The trust terminates when no living animal is covered by the trust. The instructions in the trust should state who inherits the property when the pet dies.

Other states allow a Pet Trust to be established, but the court will not enforce it. If you select the caregiver wisely you will have some assurance that the pet will receive proper care. However, the effectiveness of this arrangement turns on the reliability of the person you choose; no mechanism exists to force the caregiver to use the property for the benefit of the pet.

A large amount of money or other property left to the pet trust may cause your heirs to challenge the bequest and the court may reduce it. The trust should state how you want the funds paid and whether the caretaker should be paid for his or her services.

For obvious reasons, it may not be wise to make the person who cares for the pet the person who inherits the remainder of the funds after the pet dies.

If you want to set up a trust for your pets, it is better to do it while you are alive so that your pets will be immediately taken care of when you die (rather than through a testamentary trust). You should also fund the trust so money is available without delay. If you wish to stipulate how you want your pet buried, be sure to include these instructions within the trust.

Fact:
Enforceable Pet Trusts.

These states have modified their Uniform Probate Code and allow enforceable Pet Trusts: Alaska, Arizona, California, Colorado, Michigan, Montana, New Mexico, North Carolina and Utah. **ibutton** Pet Trusts diesmart.com/ibutton

Other states permit the establishment of pet trusts but do not require the courts to enforce their provisions.

If your state does not allow pet trusts, you should consider finding someone willing to take care of your animals when you die. You should include the identification of this person and the pets in your will or living trust. You can decide whether you want to leave money to this person for the care of your pets. There may be no legal supervision to assure that this person will take good care of your pets or spend the money on the pets.

Q. *What is a pet sanctuary?*

A. If you don't have someone willing to take care of your pets, you can consider giving your pets to a sanctuary when you die. For a set fee, the sanctuary agrees to take care of your animals during their lifetime. Many sanctuaries are connected to schools of veterinary medicine and some veterinarians are establishing animal sanctuaries.

Q. *If you are on vacation and something happens to your pet, how does the caretaker authorize medical treatment for your pet?*

A. As is the case with humans, certain medical procedures require someone to authorize the treatment. You can complete a special legal document authorizing someone to act on your behalf if you can't care for your pets, known as the Establishment of Pet Guardianship. The form identifies and authorizes someone to take care of your pets when you can't. **ibutton:** Establishment of Pet Guardianship www.diesmart.com/ibutton

$

Bottom Line:

Identify and name a guardian. Don't let the state decide when your children will inherit money and how their inheritance is managed.

Don't let your pet become a statistic, one of thousands of pets euthanized because their parents did not take care of them.

Action Checklist: Decide at what age you want your children to inherit property. Create the right plan for achieving those goals.

- ❑ Nominate a guardian of the person in case you die.
- ❑ Nominate a guardian of the person in case you become incapacitated.
- ❑ If there is someone you don't want to serve as a guardian of the person, document your reasons.
- ❑ Decide who you want to manage money on behalf of your children. Name them as a custodian. Or name them as a trustee.
- ❑ Decide when you want your minor children to inherit the money. If you want to control the age of inheritance, set up a living trust.
- ❑ If you have children with special needs, talk to a lawyer about special needs trusts.
- ❑ Set aside money and instructions for your pets.

Mistake #11: You did not act

Like it or not, death is not an option. It will happen. Once the emotions subside, your family must begin to live with the paperwork and financial aspects of your death.

Thinking about being disabled or facing our mortality can be difficult. Start somewhere. Set some short term goals and then put in place those documents which will legally create and enable what you want to have happen when you can't act for yourself.

Review the Action Checklist for the 10 mistakes that are made. Maybe you just put together a family treasure map but at least you are starting to take action.

info

Finally, laws and regulations continue to change. Make sure you review your plans on an ongoing basis. We have created www.diesmart.com to build community awareness and provide the requisite forms and documents that are referenced.

DIE $MART. It will ease the emotional and financial trauma associated with your death.

$

Bottom Line:

Dying is not just an emotional event in our life, it is a major financial event that can cost 4 to 8 percent of your net worth. Or more, if long term care is involved.

Action Checklist: Don't just die. Die smart.

- ❑ Put in place the fundamentals to avoid living probate.
- ❑ Plan around Medicare and Medicaid in the event of needing long term care assistance.
- ❑ Understand survivor benefits.
- ❑ Compare the advantages of a living trust with a will for you and your family.
- ❑ Take steps to minimize any estate taxes due.
- ❑ Understand the consequences of joint tenancy before you do it.
- ❑ Maximize the value of your tax deferred retirement accounts.
- ❑ Decide at what age you want your children to inherit property and plan accordingly.
- ❑ Create a family treasure map.

EPILOGUE

As we were going to press, my daughter's best friend, Terry, lost her mother, Rose, to lung cancer. Rose had moved from Florida to California so Terry could take care of her. It was a two year decline, and Terry found herself dealing with almost every "mistake" we have listed.

As we wrote this book, we shared with Terry what we were learning. Terry was smart; she acted on every action that applied to her situation. Rose had a modest estate. The mother of three and a housewife her entire life, her estate consisted of her house, her personal belongings, a small life insurance fund and a large pile of bills from hospice.

When Rose died, Terry knew exactly what to do. The funeral was already planned, the house was owned by a living trust naming Terry as the successor trustee. The insurance beneficiary papers were in order and within 24 hours of Rose's passing everything that needed to be done was done. Within 7 days the insurance premium came in the mail. Within two weeks, Terry had a "For Sale" sign in the front yard of her mother's house in Florida.

But best of all, Terry was able to spend the days after Rose's passing celebrating her life with her family and friends.

There were no lawyers to deal with, no probate fees, no surprises and no stress. Terry made sure that her mother Died $mart.

Other Die $mart Products.

Getting Your Affairs In Order.

A step by step guide to help you get your affairs in order. Take inventory of your estate. Calculate the probate and estate tax view of your estate and take steps to avoid probate or minimize estate taxes. Document your funeral wishes and your funeral agent. Organize legal and financial documents and facts a caregiver, executor or family member will need if you become incapacitated or when you die.

How To Arrange a Funeral.

A guide to help a family member plan and arrange a funeral. Templates you can use to create a funeral program and write an eulogy. Funeral etiquette and sample thank you cards. Optional funeral registry book.

How to Settle A Small Estate.

A guide to help a family member inventory an estate, determine if probate is required and file necessary income and estate tax returns. Includes forms and instructions to manage the distribution of non probate assets.

A Guide to Death Notifications.

A guide a family member can use to notify third parties of the death of the deceased. Who should be notified? How should they be notified? Who has the legal authority to make the notification? Includes forms and procedures to prevent the financial identify theft of the deceased.

Know Your Employee Benefit RIghts.
A federal law guarantees your right to take a leave of absence from work if you are sick or if you need to take care of a family member who is sick. This guide can help you maximize your time away from work to care for someone without jeapordizing your job or insurance coverage. The law explained in language you can understand (not just the lawyers) and use to your best advantage.

LiveSmart Eldercare.
A step by step guide for caregivers and their families. Interspersed with heartfelt personal anecdotes, LiveSmart Eldercare's guide will help readers to understand, plan and manage their caregiving responsibilities.

GLOSSARY

Account Holder: The original owner of a 401(k), Roth or other individual retirement account.

Administration: The process by which trust or probate assets are gathered ("marshaled"), inventoried, accounted for, and ultimately distributed.

Administrator: The person or financial institution that is appointed to take care of the estate of a deceased person. This term is now obsolete in Michigan and Florida. The position is now called "personal representative."

Adult: Someone who is older than the statutory definition of a minor. (i.e. In Michigan and California, a person who is 18 years of age or older.)

Advance Directive: A term that applies to any form of document that states the type of medical treatment that you want or do not want when you are unable to participate in your own decisions, or appoints someone to make your medical treatment decisions for you when you cannot. It may include a living will and a health care power of attorney.

Affidavit: A document signed under penalty of perjury asserting that the matters contained therein are true and correct. Another term to describe an affidavit is a declaration. In the context of dying smart, an affidavit is often used by the executor or personal representative to declare that they are empowered to act on behalf of the decedent.

Agent: The person you name under your durable power of attorney to make your health care and/or other decisions if you are unable to do so.

Appraised Value: The fair market value placed on assets by an appraiser, an individual who is knowledgeable about what these assets could sell for.

Assets Subject to Administration: Those assets that are subject to administration in the probate court. Sometimes these assets are referred to collectively as the "probate estate." Assets owned jointly with a surviving joint owner, life insurance proceeds and retirement plan proceeds payable to a named beneficiary other than the estate are normally not part of the administration because they are not part of the estate.

Ashes: The end product of cremation, which consists of bone fragments reduced by extreme heat and pulverization. Although some people place ashes in an urn, in many instances ashes can be stored in a plastic bag that is placed inside a sturdy plastic box. You can purchase an urn from a crematory or funeral home, or you can provide your own container for the ashes.

At Need Purchase: Decisions about funeral services made immediately after someone dies. It is referred to as an At Need purchase decision, as there is a need to dispose of the deceased within a short time frame.

Attorney-in-Fact: See Agent.

Basis: The purchase price of an asset, increased by certain transaction costs or real estate improvements used to calculate capital gains taxes.

Beneficiary: A beneficiary is a person or entity entitled to receive something, including a gift upon death, life insurance proceeds, etc.

For individual retirement accounts, the beneficiary is the person or entity the owner lists on the account form when opening up the account as the person or entity to receive the account upon the death of the owner. The named beneficiary automatically inherits the account funds when the account owner dies.

For trusts, beneficiaries may be "income beneficiaries": persons entitled to the income from one or more trust assets; they may be "principal beneficiaries": beneficiaries entitled to the principal of the asset at some specified point in time; they may be "specific beneficiaries": persons entitled to specific outright gifts of property; and/or they be "residual beneficiaries": persons entitled to the rest and remainder of the trust assets after all gifts to beneficiaries are completed.

Bonding Fee: When accepting personal responsibility for the management of someone else's financial affairs, you may be required to post a bond with the court. If you fail to perform your duties, or choose to run away with some one else's money, the bonding company will reimburse the estate the money you stole (up to the amount of the bond), and the bonding company will seek reimbursement from you.

Capital Gains: A capital gain results from the sale of something you own: stocks, bonds, or your home. It is the amount of money you receive that exceeds the cost of the asset. Capital gains are reported on your 1040 income tax return, but are taxed at a different rate than your salary.

Community Living Assistance Services and Support program (CLASS). : A program included in the Patient Protection and Affordable Care Act to help consumers pay for long term care. .

Conservator: A conservator is an adult person or institution appointed by the court and given letters documenting their legal authority and responsibility to make decisions on behalf of someone who is not considered legally able to do so, i.e., minor children or a legally incapacitated person.

Conservatorship: A conservatorship legal proceeding is required when someone is incompetent to manage his or her own financial affairs and/or personal care, and no other viable alternative legal method of delegating these duties through a durable power of attorney, living trust or other legal means exists. A legal procedure in which someone the law refers to as a conservator is appointed to manage another person's financial and/or personal affairs, referred to as a conservatee.

Conservatee: The individual named in the conservatorship papers and considered to be unable to make competent decisions for himself.

Contingent Beneficiary: A beneficiary whose gift is contingent on the happening of a certain event.

Coverdell: Coverdell accounts are educational savings accounts used to fund education.

Deceased Spouse Unused Exclusion Amount. A form enabling a surviving spouse to claim and preserve the unused portion of his or her federal estate tax exemptia surviving spouse. The Doem 706 estate tax return must be filed with the Internal Revenue Service in a timely manner.

Designated Beneficiary: A designated beneficiary is the named beneficiary on an IRA or company retirement plan beneficiary form. For tax and planning purposes, a designated beneficiary must be a person. By contract, in IRA terms, a beneficiary is not a person, but a trust, charity or the "estate."

Directive to Physicians: See Advance Directive and Living Will.

Durable Power of Attorney, or Durable Power of Attorney for Asset Management: The durable power of attorney gives someone the right to make decisions while you are incompetent.

Estate: The law refers to the assets (home, insurance, jewelry, checking accounts, 401(k)s, Roth IRAs, business interests, etc.) you own and the debts (credit cards, mortgage, etc.) you owe as your estate. Your estate includes property you own individually and property you may own as a joint owner with someone else.

Estate Recovery: The legal process a state uses to seek reimbursement from the "estate" of a deceased Medicaid recipient for all the money it spent on that recipient's care, while that person was receiving Medicaid. Different states define "estate" in different ways.

Estate Tax: A federal tax bill your estate may owe when you die if the net value of your estate is greater than the estate tax personal exemption amount allowed the year you die. Also see state inheritance taxes.

Estate Tax Rate: A percentage set by law multiplied against the taxable value of your estate to calculate the estate tax due.

Executor: The executor is the person you name in your will to act on your behalf after you die. The executor stands in the legal shoes of the decedent, and has the primary responsibility to marshal, account for and distribute the assets of the estate to the heirs. In addition, the executor is responsible for reporting and paying applicable taxes and paying creditors of the estate.

Funeral Agent: Someone you appoint and give the legal right to make choices about your body when you die.

Grantor: A person who creates and funds a trust.

Gross Value: The fair market value of all your property and financial assets, including your house, life insurance, pension plans and stocks and bonds.

Guardian: 1) The person appointed by a court to make care, custody and health care decisions for you when the court has determined that you are unable to care for yourself. 2) An adult person you nominate to take care of your minor children in the event you are unable to, or someone appointed by the court. You can name a guardian for the personal care of your minor children and you can name a guardian to manage your financial assets for the benefit of your child. This can be one person, or it can be two separate individuals.

Guardianship: A court filing to approve the appointment of a guardian. If you nominated a guardian in your will, the courts will normally appoint that person. If you did not nominate a guardian, the courts will generally follow the priority in the statues to appoint a guardian, who is generally spouse, parent, or sibling.

Health Care Declaration: See Advance Directive, Health Care Power of Attorney and Living Will.

Health Care Power of Attorney: A document in which you appoint another person to make care, custody and medical decisions if you are unable to do so.
Health Care Proxy: See Health Care Power of Attorney.

Heirs: Individuals entitled to receive a portion of a deceased person's probate estate according to a will or state intestate succession rules.

HIPPA: HIPPA stands for the Health Insurance Privacy and Portability Act and establishes federal standards and rules on how physicians can share your medical information with third parties.

HIPPA Waiver: The HIPPA Waiver form is a standard four-page form you complete designating who you authorize to see your medical records.

Inheritance Tax: Some states also have an estate tax; the state taxes are called an inheritance tax. If the state you reside in has an inheritance tax, calculations must be made to determine if your estate owes a state inheritance tax. Each state has different inheritance tax rules.

Intangible Personal Property: Property one cannot physically touch. This type of property may have some paper associated with it. Property that may be considered intangible personal property can include bank accounts, cash, stocks, bonds, mutual funds, or certificates of deposit.

Intestate: When you die without a will, the legal system refers to you as dying intestate. The intestate succession rules where you permanently reside will determine who inherits your probate assets.

Intestate Succession: The rules for distributing the probate assets of a person who died without a will. The intestate laws of the state where you reside when you die will specify who will inherit your property, as you left no instructions regarding whom you wanted to inherit your assets.

Irrevocable Living Trust: A trust that cannot be changed by anyone. Usually, a revocable trust becomes irrevocable when one of the Settlors dies.

Interment: Burial in the ground or in a tomb.

Joint Tenancy With Right Of Survivorship (JTWROS): A form of property ownership between two people where the interest of each owner automatically passes to surviving owner when the first owner dies.

Letters: Letters are documents issued by the court, as evidence of the appointment of the personal representative who has the legal authority to transact business on your behalf. If you died with a will, the letters are known as Letters Testamentary. If you died without a will, the letters are known as Letters of Administration.

Letters of Conservatorship: Legal documents signed by the judge identifying the conservator and identifying whether the conservator was granted the right to make decisions about the personal care and/or the financial estate of the conservatee. The letters of conservatorship may be shown as proof the conservator can act on behalf of the conservatee and sign legal documents on his or her behalf.

Life Expectancy Factor: The life expectancy factor for the owner of a retirement account or the beneficiary of an inherited retirement account can be found in IRS Publication 590.

- The IRS has three different life expectancy tables: Uniform Lifetime, Joint Life and Single Life. The use of a specific table is based on how the original owner or the beneficiary of a retirement account is calculating the required minimum distributions.
- Beneficiaries of inherited retirement accounts use the Single Life expectancy table to find their beginning life expectancy factor. The beginning life expectancy factor is reduced by one each year thereafter.
- The tables can be found in Publication 590 at IRSgov.com.

Living Will: Completing a Living Will, also known as an Advance Health Care Directive, accomplishes a different planning goal than completing a will. In a will, you define what should happen after you die. A living will makes it clear to doctors and family members exactly what level of care you want in the event of a catastrophic illness or accident. A living will tells doctors what kind of medical care you do or don't want if you are alive but unable to communicate.

Living Trust: A living trust is a legal document you create that goes into effect while you are living and survives after you die, and is sometimes known as an Inter Vivos (living) trust. It is usually a revocable document, meaning that the person who created the trust can make changes to it up until the time someone dies. A living trust may become irrevocable with no ability to make changes when the only person who can amend or revoke the trust dies or becomes incompetent.

Look back Period: The period of time prior to the date of a Medicaid application during which any gifts made by the person applying for Medicaid must be counted. The look back period for gifts made prior to February 8, 2006 is 36 months. The look back period for gifts made after February 8, 2006 is 60 months.

Marital Exemption: A legal structure enabling a married couple to both claim an Estate Personal Exemption Allowance.

Medicare: A federal program that pays for certain health care expenses for people aged 65 or older. Enrolled individuals must pay deductibles and co-payments, but much of their medical costs are covered by the program.

Medicaid: A program, funded by the federal and state governments, which pays for medical care for those who can't afford it. The United States federal government provides matching funds to the state Medicaid programs. State Medicaid programs may have a different name, i.e., Medi-Cal in California.

Net Unrealized Appreciation (NUA) A program allowing you as an owner of a 401(k) account to take company stock from your 401(k) plan and pay ordinary income tax on the original cost of the stock rather than on its fair market value at the time of withdrawal, assuming you elect a lump sum distribution of your 401(k) account.

Net Value of Estate: The net value of your assets is calculated by determining the fair market value of all property in your estate and making a list of the total liabilities (credit card debt, mortgage, etc.) owed. The net estate value represents the difference between the fair market value and the liabilities.

Non-Probate Assets: Certain property where the beneficiary is not determined by your will or, if you don't have a will, state intestate succession rules. Property whose title allows your ownership in the property to be legally transferred to the heirs/beneficiaries without probate supervision. Non probate assets include property held in the name of a trust, property with a beneficiary designation (IRAS, 401(k)s, life insurance, payable upon death accounts), or property jointly owned with the right of survivorship.

Patient Advocate: Under Michigan law, the person who is named in a durable power of attorney for health care who makes health care decisions for another.

Patient Surrogate: Under Florida law, the person who makes health care decisions for another. (This is the same as the Patient Advocate in Michigan.)

Principal: The person who appoints another to make decisions for him or her under a power of attorney.

Penalty Period: The term used by Medicaid to describe the period of time during which an applicant for Medicaid coverage will be disqualified from such coverage, based on the amount of gifts made within the look back period.

Pay-On-Death: A feature allowing you to name a beneficiary (or beneficiaries) for certain assets including checking accounts, savings accounts, certificates of deposit. When all the owners of the account die, the beneficiary can claim rights to the asset without probate court supervision.

Pour Over Will: A term applied to the will created when you also have a living trust. It is termed Pour Over because the will only covers property not titled and owned by the trust. A Pour Over Will provides that the assets in the probate estate are given to the trustee of the trust, and thus the assets "pour over" into the trust estate.

Probate: The judicial process used to gather, inventory, account for and ultimately distribute your assets to the people entitled to those assets after you die if the assets were held in your name at the time of death. A probate case is filed in the probate court in the county where you reside when you die. If you own real estate in more than one location, you may be required to file a probate case in each county where the real estate is located.

Probate Assets: Property that upon death passes under the provisions of a will, or, if there is no will, by intestate succession. A probate asset can require the court to supervise the transfer of title from you to the new owners. Probate assets would include property whose beneficiary is listed as "Estate" and property you own as an individual.

Probate Fees: The funds paid to open a probate case. These fees include attorney fees, court filing fees, and fees eligible to be paid to the executor or personal representative managing the probate case. Probate fees are set by state statute. Probate fees can be set as (1) a percentage of the gross value of your estate or (2) a reasonable amount.

Revocable Living Trust: A legal document you create while you are living that may be amended and/or revoked until you become incapacitated or die. The living trust survives after you die. Property owned by the trustee of the Trust is not considered a probate asset, even though the trustee is the decedent. A living trust names a successor trustee who manages the trust after you die. A co-trustee or a successor trustee can manage your assets if you become mentally incompetent or physically incapacitated without any requirement for a legal procedure.

Required Minimum Distribution (RMD): The required minimum distribution (RMD) is an Internal Revenue Service (IRS) term. RMD defines the annual amount of money required to be distributed each year by either the original owner or the beneficiary of an inherited account.

- The RMD is calculated by dividing the life expectancy of the person receiving the distribution by the amount of funds in the retirement account on December 31 of the prior year. The life expectancy factor is found in a table provided by the IRS.

- If the required RMD is not taken when required, the IRS can assess a 50% penalty.

Roboform: A software program that tracks all of your online passwords.

Rollover: The process of transferring a retirement account from one custodian to another, or changing the owner names on an account. Qualified rollovers are tax-free events.

Services of Funeral Director and Staff: Basic services that are furnished by a funeral provider in arranging any funeral, such as conducting the arrangements conference, planning the funeral, obtaining necessary permits and placing obituary notices.

Settling Your Estate: Once you die, someone you have named in your estate planning documents and/or appointed by the court takes responsibility for settling your estate. This person (a) prepares a list of things you own and determines their fair market value; (b) documents who owns the property and who the beneficiary is, identifying the property as a probate asset or a non-probate asset; (c) prepares a list of debts you owe; (d) pays your debts; (e) decides if estate taxes are due and pays them when necessary; and (g) transfers title of property to its new owners. The person in charge of your estate will also determine if probate is required.

Settlor: Another name for a grantor, someone who creates a trust.

Simple Estate: A small estate subject to an expedited court probate process. Most states have established two types of probate processes required to settle the estate of someone who dies. Usually, it is the value of the probate assets that determines which set of forms and processes is used.

Special Needs Trust: A type of trust created to distribute trust assets for the benefit of a disabled individual in such a way the trust will not disqualify the individual from receiving various government benefits.

Statutory Will: A blank form drafted by the state legislature and provided as part of a state law. If you do not want to use a lawyer to complete your will, you may consider using a statutory will.

Successor beneficiary: The term "successor beneficiary" does not apply to your other assets. It is a critical part of planning for inherited IRAs.

- When the beneficiary of your IRA sets up their inherited IRA account, your designated beneficiary can designate a successor beneficiary who will inherit the account if they die before all the funds are distributed.

Successor Trustee: The person(s) or institution that, after the initial trustee has died, becomes incapacitated or resigns, becomes the acting trustee (or co-trustee).

Tangible Personal Property: Property that you can touch, including jewelry, furniture, vehicles, golf clubs, etc.

Tenants in Common: A form of joint ownership of real estate where each owner's percentage share of the property passes according to terms in the owner's will and not to the other joint owners when each joint owner dies.

Tenants by the Entirety: A form of joint ownership of real estate where a married couple are the only owners. The surviving spouse automatically inherits the property when the first spouse dies. This type of property title is not available in all states.

Testamentary Trust: A trust that is created by your will to take effect upon your death. All property passing to a testamentary trust must go through probate.

Transfer-On-Death: A feature allowing you to name a beneficiary (or beneficiaries) for stocks and bonds. If a single individual owns the account, a TOD registration allows ownership of the account to be transferred to the designated beneficiary upon your death. For Joint Tenants with Right of Survivorship, a TOD registration transfers account ownership upon the death of the surviving account holder.

Transfer-On-Death Deed: A feature allowing you to name a beneficiary (or beneficiaries) for real estate, avoiding probate. The designated beneficiary automatically inherits the property when the owner dies. If the property is owned as joint tenants, the beneficiary inherits the property when the last tenant dies. Not available in all states.

Trust Assets: Assets owned by the trust. The trust is listed as the owner on the ownership documents, i.e., a deed, or a vehicle registration form.

Trustee: The person or financial institution named in a trust with the legal authority to manage and operate the trust. In most cases, initially, this is the person(s) who created the trust. If a married couple has a shared marital trust, they may be co-trustees.

Trustor: The person(s) who creates the trust, who is also known as the grantor or the settlor.